W9-APH-010

6.95

ON CHINESE GARDENS

by Chen Congzhou
With an Introduction by Alison Hardie

Better Link Press

Copyright © 2008 Shanghai Press and Publishing Development Company

All rights reserved. Unauthorized reproduction, in any manner, is prohibited.

This book is edited and designed by the Editorial Committee of *Cultural China* series
Adapted from *On Chinese Gardens* published by Tongji University Press in 1984

Managing Directors: Wang Youbu, Xu Naiqing
Editorial Director: Wu Ying
Editors: Yang Xinci, Zhang Yicong, Yang Xiaohe

Text by Chen Congzhou
Translation by Mao Xinyi, Wu Yiyun, Sun Li, Chen Xiongshang, Xu Zengtong and Ren Zhiji
Introduction by Alison Hardie
Photos by Chen Jianxing, IC and Gu Jianming
Interior and Cover Design: Yuan Yinchang, Li Jing

ISBN-13: 978-1-60220-102-6

Address any comments about *On Chinese Gardens* to:

Better Link Press
99 Park Ave
New York, NY 10016
USA
or
Shanghai Press and Publishing Development Company
F 7 Donghu Road, Shanghai, China (200031)
Email: comments_betterlinkpress@hotmail.com

Computer typeset by Yuan Yinchang Design Studio, Shanghai
Printed in China by Shanghai Donnelley Printing Co. Ltd.

1 2 3 4 5 6 7 8 9 10

Contents

Introduction 5

Translation of Garden Names 10

Part one Implicitness and Appropriateness 13

Part two Garden Composition 51

Part three Restoration and Renovation 81

Part four The Natural and the Cultivated 119

Part five Motion and Stillness 147

Author's Postscript 171

Index of Photographs and Illustrations 172

Dynasties in Chinese History 176

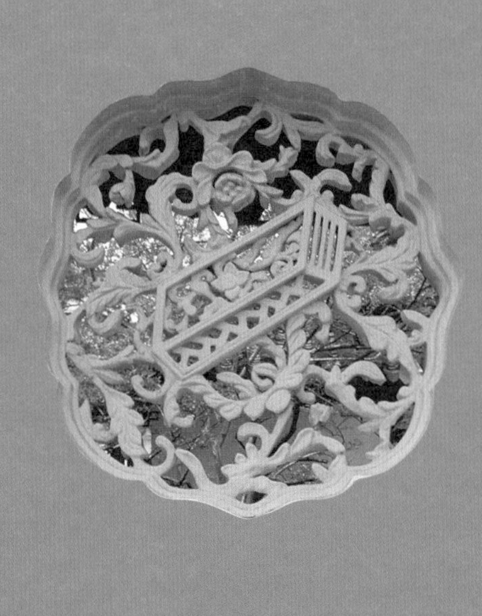

Introduction

The late Professor Chen Congzhou (1918-2000) represents a generation of Chinese scholars whose like will not be seen again. His wide-ranging and humane scholarship derived from a type of classical education which no longer exists, while his broad-minded and progressive attitude belonged to the optimistic China inspired by the May Fourth era of cultural renewal.

Chen Congzhou's family originated from the ancient city of Shaoxing in Zhejiang, a historic cultural centre, and his elegant phraseology was uttered in a marked Zhejiang accent. After graduating in 1942, during the war years, from Zhijiang University in Hangzhou, he worked in various higher education institutions including the famous St John's University in Shanghai, before moving in the early 1950s to Tongji University, where he became a professor of architecture. One of his teachers in architectural history had been the great scholar Liu Dunzhen, a pioneer in the modern study of Chinese garden history.

Chen Congzhou's contributions to the serious study of traditional Chinese gardens were immense, ranging from analyses of individual gardens or the gardens of a specific region, to studies of particular garden designers of the late imperial period. His first book on gardens, though not his first book to be published, was *Gardens of Suzhou* (*Suzhou Yuanlin*) of 1956; this was partly the outcome of personal visits to the gardens while teaching part-time in Suzhou. His collection of reading notes, published in 1997, towards the end of his life, as *Leftover Ink from the Catalpa Studio* (*Zishi Yumo*), is a treasury of quirky and fascinating pieces of information not just on gardens but on all kinds of cultural and historical subjects. As an architectural historian, he published *Draft History of Shanghai's Modern Architecture*, *The Stone Bridges of Shaoxing*, and other topics.

He was a prolific essayist and writer of occasional pieces, publishing three collections of essays on a range of subjects including gardens, many on the links between gardens and other art forms such as painting or drama. Indeed he wrote that it was kunqu, the highly refined form of Chinese music theatre, which originally sparked his interest in the art of gardens. He described hearing kunqu for the first time, as a small boy, on a record made by Yu Sulu, father of the distinguished kunqu actor Yu Zhenfei. Later, as a student, he saved money from his small allowance so that he could buy tickets to hear the young Yu Zhenfei; it was a performance of the scenes "Wandering in the Garden" and "The Startling Dream" from *The Peony Pavilion* (*Mudan Ting*) that made him realise the congruence between the underlying principles of kunqu and gardens, and the importance of comprehending their spirit as well as their form. He became a personal friend of Yu Zhenfei, who wrote the calligraphic title for *On Chinese Gardens* (*Shuo Yuan*).

Professor Chen's five essays in *On Chinese Gardens*, written between 1978 and 1982, originally published in the journal of Tongji University and then in a bilingual edition by Tongji University Press (1984), contain insights into the nature of traditional Chinese gardens derived from a lifetime's study, but are also concerned with the principles of conservation of historic landscapes and the creation of contemporary parks and gardens. Frequently, his anger and despair at ignorant or insensitive "restoration" and modernisation breaks through, always wittily and ironically expressed. Gardens in whose restoration he was himself involved, such as the Ancient Garden of Elegance (Guyiyuan) in Nanxiang, on the outskirts of Shanghai, show what can be achieved with knowledge and sensitivity.

The essays can be appreciated and enjoyed on many levels: for their humour and the elegance and fluency of their expression; for the depth of learning which they effortlessly convey; for their insights into the links between different art forms within the integrated whole of traditional Chinese culture; for the apt citation of classical literature, throwing light on various aspects of garden design and garden culture.

They also convey the ideas which Professor Chen had developed from his immersion in the subject, such as the concepts of "in-position" and "in-motion" viewing.

In the first essay, which seems originally to have been intended to stand alone, he discusses the essence of different gardens, characterising the large Zhuozheng Yuan (in Suzhou) as one suitable for in-motion viewing, and the much smaller Wangshi Yuan as one for in-position viewing. His sensitivity to traditional Chinese aesthetics leads to his appreciation of the successful design of landscapes such as the Slender West Lake in Yangzhou, as well as to the criticisms which he puts forward of unsuccessful alterations (new trees replacing old) or additions (the waterless extension to Wangshi Yuan).

He picks up the ideas of the 17th-century designers Zhang Nanyuan (Zhang Lian) and Ji Cheng, author of the *Yuan Ye*[1] (*The Craft of Gardens*) about suggesting the existence of a wider landscape through the use of partial elements of a scene, and following what is "appropriate" to a particular site. Of course, to grasp what is appropriate, the designer must already have a well-developed aesthetic sense.

The second essay relates the "composition" of gardens to other cultural forms such as poetry. This helps to explain the importance of the inscriptions which appear in Chinese gardens, often using a classical quotation to bring out the essence of a particular feature: thus the scenery is imbued with human emotions. This essay reiterates the theme of condensation and refinement raised in the first essay. It also develops the topic of appropriateness, particularly in relation to the choice of vegetation for a garden, whether large or small. Similar issues of appropriateness are raised with regard to rock work and the use of water.

The third essay is the longest of the five. Again, the art of gardens is related to classical poetry and painting, and the important role of inscriptions in the garden is emphasised. This essay is perhaps the most critical of insensitive restoration and development; this suggests that it may have been in an attempt to counteract these phenomena that Professor Chen developed his first two essays into a whole series. The essay also includes some very valuable and authoritative comments on the dating of rock work.

1. *Yuan Ye*: *The Craft of the Gardens* is the first monograph dedicated to garden architecture in the world, written in 1634 by the famous garden designer Ji Chen (1582-1637) in the Ming Dynasty.

The fourth essay is said to be based on the experiences of a year of visits to gardens and scenic areas, but the many references to writers and painters of the past, both well-known and obscure, show the extent to which Chen Congzhou's response to immediate visual stimuli was conditioned by his deep knowledge of traditional high culture. Again we find criticism of inappropriate buildings foisted on to designed landscapes, such as the cavernous Louwailou Restaurant on the West Lake.

The final and shortest essay is mainly concerned with in-motion and in-position garden viewing, originally raised in the first essay. These concepts seem to have been a contribution of Professor Chen's to Chinese garden theory; there is no mention of them, so far as I am aware, in pre-modern sources. The concepts are extended to motion (as of water) and stillness (as of rocks) within the garden, and to transition between different areas or features of a garden, the borrowing of desirable views, and the "separating" of the garden from undesirable ones (smokestacks and factories). The essay concludes with some thoughts on the importance of retaining indigenous traditions while remaining open to ideas from elsewhere.

These essays confirm that Professor Chen was very far from being a Mr Casaubon figure, immersed in abstruse and impractical scholarship. He was active in the design and conservation of traditional gardens. Moreover, he was dedicated to bringing an understanding and enjoyment of traditional garden culture to ordinary people, and a significant part of his writing was published in newspapers and popular journals. Some early pieces intended for general-interest publication are written in a self-consciously vernacular tone, in line with the emphasis on art and literature "serving the people" in the new People's Republic, but it is clear that this style did not come naturally to him; he could express himself most compellingly in the concise, allusive literary style derived from classical Chinese. This, the style of the essays *On Chinese Gardens*, presents a formidable challenge to anyone translating his work.

The Tongji University Press bilingual edition of *On Chinese Gardens* is an impressive combination of scholarship and art, with Chen Congzhou's elegant Chinese prose presented in fine calligraphy by his old friend and relative Jiang Qiting (with whom he collaborated on the posthumously published anthology *Yuanzong* [2004]), preceded by Yu Zhenfei's vigorous title; the English translations, by various hands, are generally of remarkably high quality.

Anyone doing research on traditional Chinese gardens owes Professor Chen an incalculable debt for his scholarly publications and his guidance to subsequent generations of students. I count myself very fortunate to have met him once, and to have had the benefit of hearing his views on Ji Cheng and the *Yuan Ye*. He lives on in all our memories as a true scholar and gentleman.

Alison Hardie
University of Leeds
U.K.
February 2007

Translation of Garden Names

古猗园	Guyi Yuan, Nanxiang, Shanghai	Ancient Garden of Elegance
别峰庵	Bie Feng An, Zhenjiang	Another Peak Nunnery
拙政园	Zhuozheng Yuan, Suzhou	The Artless Administrator's Garden
个园	Ge Yuan, Yangzhou	The Bamboo Garden
卷石洞天	Quan Shi Dong Tian	Cave Heaven of the Fist-sized Rock
耦园	Ou Yuan, Suzhou	The Couple's Garden Retreat
东园	Dong Yuan, Suzhou	The East Garden
艺圃	Yi Pu, Suzhou	The Garden of Cultivation
颐和园谐趣园	Xiequ Yuan at Summer Palace, Beijing	The Garden of Harmony
怡园	Yi Yuan, Suzhou	The Garden of Joy
汴园	Bian Yuan, Kai Feng, Henan Province	The Garden of Kaifeng
听风园	Tingfeng Yuan, Suzhou	The Garden for Listening to the Breeze
寄畅园	Jichang Yuan, Wuxi, Jiangsu Province	The Garden for Lodging One's Expansive Feelings
豫园	Yu Yuan, Shanghai	The Garden of Pleasure
退思园	Tuisi Yuan, Suzhou	The Garden of Withdrawal for Contemplation
何园	He Yuan, Yangzhou, Jiangsu Province	The He Family Garden
留园	Liu Yuan, Suzhou	The Lingering Garden
狮子林	Shizi Lin, Suzhou	The Lion Forest Garden

蠡园	Li Yuan, Wuxi	Fan Li's Garden
西湖柳浪闻莺	Liu Lang Wen Ying, the West Lake, Hangzhou	Listening to the Orioles by the Willow Waves
网师园	Wangshi Yuan, Suzhou, Jiangsu Province	The Master of the Nets Garden
环秀山庄	Huanxiu Shan Zhuang, Suzhou	Mountain Villa Surrounded by Greenery
近园	Jin Yuan, Changzhou, Jiangsu Province	Near Garden
北麓园	Beilu Yuan, Nantong, Jiangsu Province	The Northern Foothills Garden
秋霞圃	Qiuxia Pu, Jiading, Shanghai	Nursery-garden of Autumn Vapours
圆明园	Yuanming Yuan, Beijing	Old Summer Palace
瞻园	Zhan Yuan, Nanjing, Jiangsu Province	The Outlook Garden
珍珠泉	Zhenzhu Quan, Jinan, Shandong Province	The Pearl Spring
十笏园	Shihu Yuan, Weifang, Shandong Province	Shihu Garden
瘦西湖	Shou Xi Hu, Yangzhou	The Slender West Lake
净心斋	Jingxin Zhai, Bei Hai, Beijing	The Studio for Cleansing the Heart
颐和园	Yihe Yuan, Beijing	Summer Palace
沧浪亭	Canglang Ting, Suzhou	The Surging Waves Pavilion
碧霞寺	Bixia Temple, Tai Mountain, Shandong Province	Temple of Azure Vapours
雷峰塔	Leifeng Pagoda, Hangzhou, Zhejiang Province	Thunder Peak Pagoda
虎丘	Hu Qiu, Suzhou	Tiger Hill

Part One

Implicitness

AND

Appropriateness

Chinese garden design has a long history and has developed a distinctive character of its own. Scholars have analysed and discussed it from a variety of perspectives and stated their views. I should like to offer some observations on gardens with which I am familiar, and will call my essay *On Chinese Gardens*.

Chinese gardens may be divided into two kinds: those for "in-position viewing" i.e. lingering observation from fixed angles, and those for "in-motion viewing" i.e. moving observation from changing angles. This must be the first and foremost consideration before constructing a garden. The former means that there are more visual points of interest to appreciate from fixed angles, while the latter demands a longer "touring" vista. In small-scale gardens, the former type should be predominant

and the latter secondary and the reverse should be the case in large-scale gardens. An example of the former type is Wangshi Yuan, and of the latter Zhuozheng Yuan. In Wangshi Yuan, you will discover many buildings in which you would love to sit and linger awhile. You can make a tour of the pond, you can stand by the balustrade and count the swimming fish, or you can seat yourself in the pavilion to wait for the moon and greet the breeze. Outside the veranda the shadows of flowers move along the walls, and looking out through a window there are ridges and peaks like those in a painting. The serenity of the scene is enchanting. In Zhuozheng Yuan, paths wind around a pond, and long corridors draw the visitors ahead. The pond looks like The Slender West Lake, where "gaily-decorated pleasure boats glide to and fro under the bridge at midday and visitors can catch glimpses of scented garments." The view changes with every step. This is what is meant by a design for observation from changing angles. First comes the conception, then the design and then the construction. Adequate attention must be paid to the character and area of the garden. The potted landscape (bonsai) garden currently being built in Shanghai is a suitable example of a garden mainly for viewing from fixed angles.

Chinese gardens, with their buildings, landscaping and different kinds of flowers and trees, are integrated works of art, lyrical and picturesque. The overall appearance, though man-made, should appear to be formed by nature. What is the actual relationship between hills and waters in a garden? Briefly, when imitating natural landscapes, parts of a particular scene should be chosen rather than taking an entire scene in miniature (extremely well done in the imitation of the White Lotus Pool on the Tiger Hill in Suzhou in Wangshi Yuan), and the principles of disposition should follow those of paintings. Hills are valued for their veins and waters for their sources, and if these are properly set out, the whole garden will come to life. In describing the relationship between hills and waters I have used these words, "The waters follow the hills, and the hills are brought to life by the waters", and "streams meander because of the hills, and paths follow the terrain." I've derived a great deal of inspiration from real mountains and rivers. Zhang Nanyuan, a late Ming-early Qing rockery designer, advocated using flat terraces, mild slopes and small hills and mounds to make the garden closely resemble the natural world. If we can grasp this principle and do not stray too

far from nature then this ideal state, the perfect harmony of waters and rocks, will emerge.

Trees are planted in Chinese gardens not only for their foliage but also for their aesthetic appeal. A corner of flowers and trees outside a window presents a scene of truncated branches. A couple of aged

trees and a clump of secluded bamboos are modelled on paintings of "withered trees, bamboos, and rocks". The emphasis is placed on their aspect and not on their type. As with potted landscapes, each scene can be taken as a work of art. The maples and willows of Zhuozheng Yuan and the ancient cypresses of Wangshi Yuan are outstanding sights in these gardens. The beauty of the gardens would certainly be lessened by removing these ancient trees. In the past there were numerous lacebark pines in Liu Yuan, pines and plums in Yi Yuan, and bamboos at the Canglang Ting, and each had its own distinctive character. But in recent years this has not been paid proper attention to (here we should take heed), and different species have all been mixed together, with the result that the individual character of these gardens has been much reduced. Guo Xi, a famous landscape painter of the Song Dynasty in 11 century, said it well, "With hills think of the streams as their veins, the grass as their hair, and the mists and clouds as their expressions."If this is true of grass, it is even more so of trees. I have always felt that a garden should reflect the distinctive character of a particular area, and that local trees retain their vitality and grow more quickly, becoming dense growth in

a few years. This type of garden differs from botanical gardens, because it lays emphasis on the view and not on the quantity or outlandishness of the plants. "A garden excels because of its scenery and scenery varies with different gardens." This is of course also true of flowers. Each Chinese garden has a style of its own, seeking difference in similarity and similarity in difference. Classical gardens devoted much time to creating a style in which pavilions, terraces, and storeyed buildings as well as hills, rocks, and ponds would look different in wind or with flowers, in snow or in moonlight and would always seem new and fresh.

We Chinese people have a particular approach to art appreciation — for instance, with flowers and trees the emphasis must be placed on their posture, in music on the melody, in painting and calligraphy on the brushwork and conception. All require painstaking work in order to produce pieces that you will never get tired of looking at and listening to, and that will bear rigorous examination and make a pleasing impression. Exploration of our national styles will greatly inspire us.

There are two types of garden scenery: that which offers a panoramic vista and that for viewing at close range, and in handling this, we should deal with each case differently. Storeyed buildings, forbidding rocks and winding streams all reflect this principle."A small red pavilion stands by a small red bridge, thousands of cicadas sing in the tall willows, by the red

pavilion." "In the shadow of green willows, by the side of the Crabapple Pavilion, are the tips of pink apricots." These lines not only describe registers of scenery, producing a sense of space and sound, but also lead the observers' vision upward to the tall willows and along to the tips of apricot branches. Our gardeners should cultivate this scholars' sensibility. "A hill with hidden winding paths and a hundred steps conquered at a slow pace" talks about viewing scenery at a close range while passing

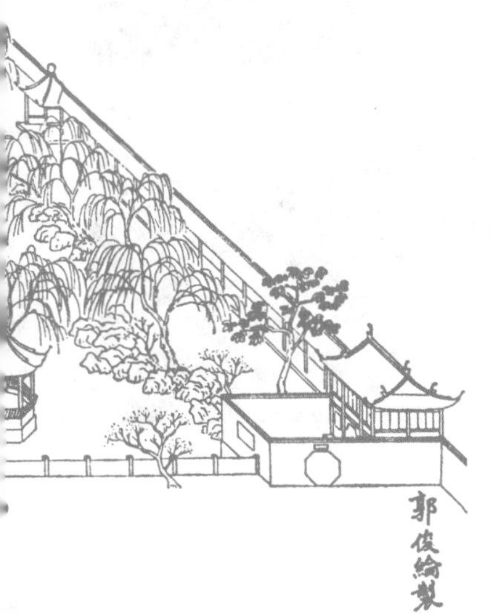

by. Therefore, we should not take any hasty action, but should design the roofs of buildings, the base of a rockery, the ingress and egress of waters, and the tips of trees carefully. To set a pavilion in the hills or to place rocks jutting out into the water are methods of drawing the vision from both higher and lower angles.

Why is it that China's scenic places and classical gardens attract countless visitors and one can view them over a hundred times without ever being satiated? No doubt the beauty of the scenery is an important reason, but culture and history are other key factors. I've already mentioned that objects of cultural interest and historic sites enrich scenic spots and gardens, and produce even greater pleasure and broader associations in visitors, who will not then come merely to sightsee, eat and take a cup of tea. When cultural objects are combined with scenic places or gardens, the preservation of the former can be ensured, and the latter can be enriched and variegated. They complement one another, and are unified rather than dissonant. In this way a socialist Chinese garden which reflects both ancient and modern culture can be achieved.

The Chinese garden is wonderful for its implicitness, for the way in which a hill or rock can evoke contemplation. An upright peak is a piece of abstract sculpture. The Beautiful Woman Peak requires careful

observation before one can see the resemblance. This is also true of the Nine Lions Mountain. The front and back beam frames of the Mandarin Duck Hall are shaped differently, but somebody has to drop a hint before you suddenly realize that it contains an image of an affectionate couple. There are, however, well-intentioned people who, afraid that visitors might not understand what is presented before them, place large man-made fish in ponds or clay pandas in front of a Panda Hall like large advertisements. This is the antithesis of implicitness, destroying the spirit of Chinese gardens and ruining the scenery. Fish should fleetingly

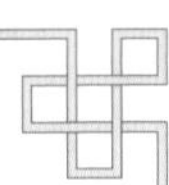

appear and disappear, and a Panda Hall will seem even more intriguing amidst clumps of bamboo. Then the visitors will appear to be entering a wonderland and their interest will be aroused. In the past, certain gardens, such as the Han Bi[1] Mountain Villa, the Plum Garden, and Wangshi Yuan, were all just what their names implied; their special features were lacebark pines, plum blossoms and waters respectively. A still better example is provided by the famed Ten Sceneries of the West Lake at Hangzhou. The inscribed tablets placed on pavilions, houses and terraces offer suggestions on how to enjoy the scenery. Go, for example, to the pavilion named He Feng Si Mian Ting, The Pavillion where One Enjoys the Fragrance of Lotus from All Four Sides. The place induces a contemplative mood, and though there may not in reality be any breeze, you still feel as though there was wind everywhere. You will be overcome with admiration, and walk back and forth reading the absorbing couplets and beautiful calligraphy. At Zheng Banqiao's study in "Another Peak Nunnery" at the summit of Mount Jiao, there are numerous flowering trees and three small rooms. When visitors read the couplet on the door "A tasteful room need not be large and fragrant flowers need not be many", they will feel at peace, see the particular appeal of the scenery and will all praise it. The horizontal inscriptions are on brick or stone tablets and the couplets are carved on wooden panels, bamboo slats, wooden screens, or on slabs of marble. These are more effective in provoking contemplation than more detailed images, since Chinese gardens are like artistic compositions; their quality is enhanced more by suggested lines and by abstract marble forms than by concrete images.

1. Han Bi (cold jade) is a poetic name for the lacebark pine.

玉壺冰
曲水崇山雅集逾獅林虎阜

Paper, which is easily damaged, is generally not used. Therefore, on the doors and walls of buildings, couplets are inscribed on brick, stone, bamboo, or wooden panels depending on local conditions. In the halls and studies of a residence, calligraphies and paintings intensify the effect of light and sound and produce a feeling of clarity and serenity. At one time there were standard sizes of *xuan* paper[1] and the sizes of mounts for calligraphy and painting were standardized according to the dimensions of buildings.

In Chinese gardens there is a relationship between the winding and the straight. The winding exists within the straight and vice versa, and they should appear to co-exist naturally and with ease. Painters have said that when depicting a tree they ought never to make a line that is not curved. This is considered one of the basic techniques of painting. Winding bridges, paths, and corridors were originally intended to facilitate communication between places. The garden is landscaped on all sides and if the designer plans curving paths instead of straight ones the visitors will be surrounded by pleasant scenery. The route will seem longer and more interesting. Thus it can be seen that curving lines are derived from straight ones and that their design should follow certain rules. Some zigzagging bridges are constructed with nine curves but are not close to the surface

1. A high quality paper made in Xuancheng, Anhui Province.

of the pond (in general, garden bridges ought to be lower than the pond's banks in order to evoke a feeling of being above the waves). They can seem awkward and make visitors feel uneasy while walking across. This is because of an inadequate understanding of theory (the old zigzag bridge in the Yu Yuan of Shanghai was a bad example of this).

When the location has been settled, thought must be given to the terrain and to the main characteristics of the garden in order to achieve the desired effects. Yuanming Yuan in Beijing is set against a lake and the Western Hills. It is laid out in relation to the lake and to the Western Hills, and has become "a garden of ten thousand gardens". Jichang Yuan in Wuxi is set in foothills. Designed to face the mountains, it incorporates them into its scenery. Wangshi Yuan is designed around a pool. Although there are no natural waters in Dianchun Yi, at its southwest corner is a cool fountain which links together all of the waterways in the whole garden and gives it life. However, the newly-built eastern part of the garden violates the original design. Moreover, the absence of water has brought the scenery to a stalemate. This is the result of inadequate analysis and careful consideration at the outset.

Ideal gardens are like superb lines of verse. They are so designed as to make "few" seem to surpass "many" and to evoke a sense of infinity, the way a plucked note reverberates between beam frames (large-scale gardens are apt to be overlooked at points in the way that lengthy songs and slow tunes are difficult to sing in one breath). What I have said about "gardens outside gardens" and "scenery outside scenery" means just this. "Scenery outside gardens" depends on "borrowing", and "scenery outside scenery" on "time". The shadows of flowers, trees, clouds and

waters, the sound of wind and water, the singing of birds and the fragrance of flowers, all join visible and invisible settings into a symphony. And these are all closely linked to poetic sentiment and artistic conception.

It is difficult to feel compact in a spacious garden and spacious in a small garden of only a few *mu*. When a garden is compactly laid out, it does not induce a feeling of spaciousness in visitors and they thus do not tire of walking in it. Neither do they feel cramped and they can take everything in. Therefore, gardens with views for both "in-position" and "in-motion" viewing can make the area seem to contract or expand. They appear to have been drawn with bold brushes and a careful finish (to use the language of painters) and so written that open spaces seem so broad that horses could gallop in them and narrow places so narrow that even a needle could not be inserted (to use the language of calligraphers). Therefore, in the Summer Palace in Beijing there is

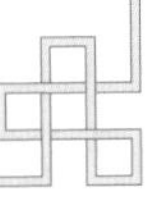

the broad expanse of misty Kunming Lake as well as Xiequ Yuan hidden deep in the hills. We can thus realize why things should be so. In garden design there are rules but no fixed formulas and what is important is the inventive application of these rules. The "use of the setting" (adaptation to local conditions, and borrowing scenery), as Ji Cheng said, is the rule. Even *Yuan Ye* has no formulas. Making a distinction between large and small gardens, between in-position and in-motion viewing, country and city gardens, is known as doing what is "appropriate". Chinese paintings of orchids or bamboos may seem rather simple, but each artist has a style of his own. With selected scenes from classical Chinese operas, which are always a delight to watch, each actor performs differently, each with originality. The theory of garden design is the same. Should a student

take only one classical model, it would be as though one used only *The Mustard Seed Garden Manual* in painting and "eight-legged essays" in writing. Wangshi Yuan in Suzhou, recognized as the finest example of the small-scale garden, is an instance of "small and fine, and few surpassing many". The design principle of contrast and interdependence of artificial rock formations and buildings is quite simple (All of the Suzhou gardens have fundamentally adopted this method. The new eastern section of Wangshi Yuan goes against this principle and is unsuccessful artistically). No boat-like structures, no large bridges or large hills, the right number

of buildings, all done on a small scale — this is the pattern of a small garden. In Shizi Lin (the Lion Forest Garden) a large boat structure was added, with improper proportions between boat and water. This was not "appropriately" set. There is poem on rehabilitating Wen Yuan by the Qing scholar Wang Chuntian, which says, "To change garden fences, and repair stone banisters — improving a garden is more difficult than correcting a poem. We should be able to chant every word properly and with feeling, even a small pavilion and small terrace can provide much food for thought." Even today, garden designers are moved reading this poem.

Garden dimensions are relative, not absolute. Without "large" there is no "small", and vice versa. The more sparsely a garden is laid out, the more spacious it feels and the more changes there are, thus creating a sense of boundless space within a limited area. "Small gardens encircled by large gardens" is based on this principle (San Tan Yin Yue, Three Pools Mirroring the Moon, in the West Lake, is an example of a large lake encircling small ones). There are many such examples, and this principle has been adopted by most garden makers. Masterpieces, such as the Loquat Garden and the Flowering Crabapple Castles of Zhuozheng Yuan and the Xiequ Yuan at the Summer Palace have all reached a very high artistic level. If at the entrance to a garden you find it big, flat, and poorly set out, you will not feel like walking through it. If a landscape has its own special features and beauty and grace, then visitors will not be content to go once but will want to make further visits. Is it not a good thing that visitors are not satisfied with seeing a garden once but yearn to visit it many times? I feel sad at the thought of many scenic

places which, in order to enable visitors to take in everything at a glance, provide them with more room and to accommodate day or even half-day visits, have had some of their walls removed to make themselves seem more spacious, although in fact they seem deserted and plain. This has been the result at the "Ping Hu Qiu Yue, Autumn Moon on the Calm Lake" and the "Xi Ling Yin She, Xi Ling Seal-cutting Society" gardens at the West Lake. The Ge Mountain Range has been dwarfed by the construction of the Xi Ling Guest House. The Slender West Lake of Yangzhou is wonderfully named because of the word "slender", and it shows foresight that there will be no tall buildings beside it. Originally, this scenic area was a group of private gardens. Its best feature is that all of the gardens give onto the water and have a distinctive style, separately constructed but harmoniously blending with towers in neighbouring courtyards and pink apricots hanging over walls mirrored in the water like paintings. Although "slender", the landscape is serene and graceful. It does not look shabby in the least. However one blemish in an otherwise perfect creation is that the garden is not compact enough. And there are too few major buildings. When it is restored, its original character should be preserved. Now that Zhuozheng Yuan is merged with the East Garden, the original area seems more cramped in spite of its enlargement and the East Garden is too big to sustain visitors' interest and so they treat it as a passageway. Obviously, to separate them was beneficial to both and to merge them a gain to neither.

Originally, Chinese wooden

structures had their individuality and their limitations; palaces, halls and pavilions each had their own style and layout. They were all built according to specific proportions. If the proportions were off, then the structure would be nondescript. If the plan was not adequate, buildings could be joined together, the way Islamic mosques are connected by corridors. In the eastern part of Zhuozheng Yuan, a pavilion has been enlarged, but it now looks neither like a gazebo nor a pavilion. It is an unpleasant sight and visitors have raised many complaints about it. The Five-Pavilion Bridge and the White Pagoda of the Slender West Lake are both imitations of the Great Bridge, the Five

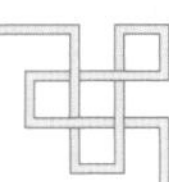

Dragon Pavilion and the White Pagoda in Beihai Park in Beijing. Owing to insufficient space, bridge and pavilions are merged, and the White Pagoda is also correspondingly reduced in scale in order to integrate with the lake and set off its special characteristics. It would be impossible not to call the Slender West Lake a fine work of art. It has been very adequately executed. Without careful scrutiny, it can hardly be recognized as a miniature of Beihai's scenery.

One should see no base with distant mountains, no roots in distant forests, and no hulls of distant ships (only their sails should be visible) — this is a principle of painting, and also a principle of garden design. From any point in the garden, a different picture should be presented. The scenery is graduated and has depth. "Leaning on a balustrade, I often look lingeringly over the water. To prevent anything obscuring the mountains, no walls are built around", if these principles — to conceal what should be concealed, to screen what should be screened, to widen openings, separate what should be separated, divide what should be divided, and so on — are applied, then only parts and not the whole can be seen. There will seem to be pictures outside pictures, and a foot will seem like a thousand *li*. All this lingers pleasantly in the mind. In concrete terms, pavilions should be erected at a place a little down from the top of the mountain, trees should not be planted on the mountain peak, a mountain may show its foot or its top but not both, and likewise a large tree may show its top or its roots but not both, etc. Application of these principles is a matter of careful and long deliberation. Even the pruning of a tree or the removal of a stone will influence the appearance of a landscape. Making a mistake over even one branch of a tree could spoil a whole garden. The old tree behind the Magnolia Hall in Zhuozheng

Yuan withered and has been replaced by a new one now, but this has destroyed the former balance. The front of the Quxi Tower in Liu Yuan has suffered the same fate. From this I can fully see that garden management is as difficult as garden design. A good gardener should not only study the history of the garden but should also familiarize himself with its artistic characteristics. He is just like a competent nurse who gives her patients all of her care and understanding. In particular, important protected cultural sites should not be rashly repaired. They must be repaired in accordance with the original form. No unauthorized changes should be made. Otherwise, not only would the style of the garden be spoiled but the site would also suffer as a consequence.

Gardens in suburbs have a more rural aspect, while gardens attached to residences are valued for their purity and freshness. The rural type is closer to nature; to be pure and fresh is to be unconventional. Li Yuan in Wuxi is an example of vulgarity and does not induce any sense of the country, while Wangshi Yuan can be considered a model of purity and freshness. Although the former is a garden of great size, there have been very few positive comments on it. The latter, though small, is constantly praised. This proves that a garden succeeds on its quality rather than on

its size. Quality is what determines artistic excellence. Not only should consideration be given to style, but care should also be exercised with regard to different fittings and furnishings. The decoration of a garden should be carried out in accordance with local conditions. The lines and contours of open buildings should be beautifully wrought and need no hanging decorations, which are easily damaged. All items of furniture, such as stone benches and tables and tiled tables, should be made in a traditional style. The windows and doors of halls and verandas should be

finely decorated. Articles of furniture in rosewood, sandalwood, *nanmu* or piebald pear, should be made to match. To meet the needs of different seasons, chairs should be cane-seated in summer and cushioned in winter. Different types of furnishing should be used in sumptuous and in simple buildings. The former should be furnished with rosewood or sandalwood articles, the latter with articles of *nanmu* or piebald pear. The same is true of sophisticated and simple carvings. The furniture of a room is often referred to as its "internal organs". It cannot be denied that a garden without furniture is like a man without learning. All this is a matter of taste. In setting out the furniture of Wangshi Yuan a lot of time and energy was expended to bring it to a high level, so as to enable visitors to gain a comprehensive understanding of the art of Chinese garden design.

In ancient times night visits to gardens decorated with lanterns were great occasions, often described in poetry and literature. The actual hanging of the lanterns was a great event. Many priceless lanterns would be hung temporarily, then removed and stored away, not fixed permanently. Since lanterns are a part of the garden, their make and hang, as with screens and couplets, should be in accord with the overall design and specific character. In some gardens now there are electric lights for night visits, but this usually spoils the style of the garden. For example, the Shan Juan Cave in Yixing, full of bright, contrasting colours, now looks just like a cafeteria, and you wonder whether or not it is even a natural cave. Having the ridge corners of the pavilions in Shizi Lin decorated with electric lamps makes a shocking sight. Whether ancient buildings, classical gardens or places of scenic beauty, they should be handled with circumspection, and disharmonic

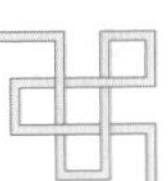

elements should be imposed on them as rarely as possible. As regards illumination, I think lights should be hidden from view unless they are for decoration, when they can be more conspicuous. In addition, their shapes should be in harmony with the buildings. The location should vary depending on whether a building is open or enclosed. Ingeniously and finely made lanterns are not suitable for open corridors exposed to draughts. Like pagoda bells, they swing in the wind and are liable to be damaged. Nor should they be hung at random. More attention should be paid to electricity wires and poles, which not only spoil a garden's scenery but also block lines of vision and are a great nuisance to photographers.

The foregoing trifling statements, although they are mundane and are apt to bore readers, are nevertheless not harmful. For the improvement of our art and the flourishing of our culture, I have here set forth my humble beliefs for reference.

Translated by Mao Xinyi

Part Two

Garden Composition

Another term for the making of a garden is garden composition. There is much in the word composition. Garden composition is by no means a mere matter of setting up halls and pavilions and planting trees and flowers. It involves deep contemplation and aesthetic appeal. Just read the great poet Du Fu's[1] "*Ten Poems on Accompanying Mr. Zheng Guangwen to visit General He's Mountain Forest*"and "*Five Poems on Revisiting He's Garden*". As the poet toured the place with his friend, he composed poems, describing the scenery in the garden and the visitors in the scenery. The figures integrated well with the scenery and the scenery varied with different visitors. "The famed garden lies by the green waters, and wild bamboos rift the blue skies"; "The bamboos bending, the wind tears off the shoots, and nourished by raindrops, the plums turned red." These lines depict the scenery in the garden. "The master's interest has been aroused and the grounds are left untended. Casually, I sat down, and found myself in the midst of berries and moss.""Leaning forward to dip my brush into the inkstone on the balustrade, I put down the poems on the Chinese parasol leaves before me." Here the lines depict the visitors in the scenery. Thus we can see that there is something common between the composition of a poem and that of a garden. Only with such an artistic conception can we understand the principles of garden composition.

1. Du Fu: 712-770, great poet of the Tang Dynasty.

Wind, flowers, snow and the moon exist in the objective world. If a garden composer "has these at his beck and call" and makes an ingenious use of them, he will be able to set off the aesthetic charm of a classical garden. In the Wangshi Yuan of Suzhou there is a pavilion, known as The Wind and the Moon Rise Together, facing west on the pond. The pavilion, with its whitewashed walls that look like screens, embraces the beauty — the quintessence — of the scenery. Thus the wind and the moon are at the disposal of the garden composer. In the case of Three Pools Mirroring the Moon in the West Lake, the pools are the finishing touches, for without

the pools there would be no beauty of the scenery
what we call "adding the finishing touches to the s
painted dragons on the temple wall, the dragons br
and soared right into the clouds when the artist painted pupils in their eyes as a finishing touch. Here the same principle operates.

Sometimes "the beauty of the scenery is viewed without any mention of it". Only when an inscription is added to it, is the splendor of the scenery unveiled. In the chapter *The Testing of Literary Talent by Composing Plaque Inscriptions in Grand View Garden* (the seventeenth chapter of *A Dream of Red Mansions*), is described how, after the completion of the construction work in Grand View Garden, inscriptions on tablets were required to be made for the various pavilions, terraces and storeyed buildings in it. It says, "If no inscriptions on tablets are made for the several pavilions and halls in the Garden with such splendid

views, even flowers, willows, hills and ponds will fail to add color to it." Hence inscriptions are designed to bring out the scenery. One has to "search for scenery" before he can compose an inscription — that is, to linger at those points of interest, observe and contemplate carefully. Jiang Taoshu of the Qing dynasty had these lines:

I'll certainly look foolish to search for a poem.
I can't very well refuse if it thrusts itself upon me.
Nevertheless the poem has again found me today.
Waters and hills in bygone days reappear before my eyes.

Only when you are in such a mood can you finish off your inscription with inspiration.

In ancient times garden construction usually started with buildings. In constructing a private garden, a sophisticatedly decorated hall as a rule was built before trees and rocks were laid out. Very often attempts would be made to tear down or break up what had been put up, and much effort thrown in to rebuild the dismantled parts and improve upon them. The whole process would be repeated several times until the desired effect was achieved. Shen Yuanlu in Qin Dynasty once wrote *About Guyi Yuan*: "It is the hall that dominates the garden in its grandeur; and it is the hill that excels in appearance." In a classical garden, buildings come first,

while trees and rocks are only ornaments and are therefore of secondary importance. However, the approach is different now. Today the common practice is to dig ponds and pave paths before the construction of the main buildings. It often happens that huge sums of money are spent while the garden remains only half finished and the visitors can find no place to step in. A reversal in priorities and the garden becomes a bare garden. To grow more trees, quite a few landscape gardens, health resorts, scenic spots and places of historic interest have been made to look like nurseries for the old trees there were cut down and replaced by new ones and yet the superintendents flatter themselves that they are "keeping a nursery garden within a garden." This is certainly preposterous!

Apart from "searching for scenery", the garden should be so laid out as to draw visitors to its highlights. Since the collapse of Leifeng Pagoda the scenery on the Southern Hill has become bare and lifeless. The scenery becomes lively when it is inspired with sentiments, and sentiments find their source in human beings. "Fragrant grass is not without sentiments. The setting sun whispers not a word. Wild geese are moving slowly in a line high above and across the south river. Figures can be seen leaning on the West Balcony." No balcony, no figures; no figures, no sentiments; no sentiments, no scenery. Obviously, the balcony is the key to the scenery. From this we can see the role buildings are subjected to in landscape gardens as well as in places of scenic beauty.

In former times, garden designers always conceived plans for their landscape. Only those plans that had given a great deal of thought to the local surroundings displayed much originality. Near the West Lake there was a path leading from Manjiaolong to a secluded retreat closed

in by hills. Groves of sweet-scented osmanthus were to grow here so that the fragrance of the flowers permeated and stayed. Moreover, the gurgling springs, the misty mountain air helped to moisten the flowers and intensify the fragrance. No wonder visitors found it a great delight to go and enjoy the sweet-scented osmanthus there on an autumn day when they rambled about the place at a leisurely pace, intoxicated and reluctant to leave. Now I hear a highway has been opened up which sends up clouds of dust as cars speed across the broad surface. The scenery is ruined as a consequence. As for plants in small-scale gardens, those with scented blossoms should be fenced in, and banana trees should be planted at the foot of a wall or near the corners of a building as their outstretched green leaves fall easy victims to the wind, and peonies should be placed to the south of the main hall as they flourish in the sun. Therefore, attention should be directed as to whether the plants are to be exposed or sheltered.

The merit of the potted landscape (bonsai) lies in that one sees the large through the small. "Tiny trees grow sturdy and strong in the small pots. Green is seen at the reduced peaks." Ingenuity is revealed here in the layout. But now landscape in the pot has been made to appear larger and larger, just like an elephant shut in a canary cage. There are things

that are indispensable to a potted landscape, namely: plants, a pot and a lattice. Potted landscapes should be viewed from fixed angles and in solitude too.

Most of our gardens in ancient times were enclosed ones with a view to creating a sense of infinite space within a limited area. Hence "spaciousness" and "flexibility" are the gist of garden designing. With flowers and trees the emphasis is placed on their posture; but with hills and rocks much importance is attached to the setting of hillocks and gullies. "Condensation" and "refinement" are characteristics of the Chinese garden, which is so laid out as to invariably produce an effect of making "the few" surpass "the many". There used to be an antithetical couplet written on a pair of scrolls hanging on either side of the stage of a theatre which read: "Three or five steps make a journey across the country; six or seven men represent a host of an army." Such are the principles of performing traditional Chinese opera. The same is true of garden construction.

Lacebark pines rank first among the trees planted in Chinese gardens.

With their simple and plain trunks, sparse and elegant foliage, they have the appearance of grown trees in spite of their adolescence. Poplars and willows, which frequently appeared in ancient Chinese poems, are seen fit to adorn gardens. There was even a Ten Thousand Willows Garden. But they are rarely found in gardens south of the Changjiang (Yangtze) River. Willows do not fit in small-scale gardens because they must be planted by water in threes or fives with foliage and twigs densely woven like a heavy curtain so that light can hardly penetrate. In Northern China a garden generally covers a large area where tall willows reach the clouds while their long twigs, graceful and gentle, kiss the pond with tenderness — all this bringing additional charm to the garden. So concrete analysis should be made with each individual case and no hard and fast rules should be laid down. Some say no willows should grow in gardens in Southern China because big catkin willows tend to wither soon, which fact has been seen as an ill omen. If this were true, how come there was the scene "The Path Meanders in the Shadows of the Willows" in the Zhuozheng Yuan of Suzhou?

Trees in places of scenic beauty all have local color. Take pines for example. There are the Tianmu Mountain pine, the Yellow Mountain

pine, the Tai Mountain pine and so on, all of which adapt themselves to the local conditions and label the natural beauty of the scenery in the different mountains. Now, there have emerged quite a few "modern" garden designers who seek to beautify the landscape of our motherland by "making foreign things serve China." They have taken great pains indeed. Consequently, cerdar can be found in almost every Chinese classical garden just like penicillin which has been regarded as a kind of panacea and used indiscriminately. "Crows may find hiding places in willows at White Gate (Nanjing)." "City overgrown with green willows features the famed Yangzhou." But now catkins no longer fly from the aged willows, and cerdar have settled into every home. Formerly, Mount Tai was famous for and characterized by the Tai Mountain pines. Today, however, cerdar pines are seen even in Dai Temple.[1] Thus decorated, the classical garden is like an ancient Chinese in a western-styled suit and a pair of modern leather shoes. An appropriate description of this will be "the thing is neither fish nor fowl."

In the setting out of pavilions, terraces and storeyed-buildings as well as hills, rocks and ponds, Chinese gardens attach much importance to local style which varies immensely with different places. Formerly in the

1. A temple dedicated to Mount Tai, the sacred mountain of the East.

Lingnan gardens (gardens south of the Five Ridges, the area covering Guangdong and Guangxi provinces) the storeyed buildings were hemmed in by the garden walls, and visitors felt an exquisite coolness in the shades of the towering trees and the deep ponds. The refreshing winds blowing into the waterside halls removed the sweltering summer heat instantly. Now and then the shadows of bamboos fell on the visitors and the fragrance of orchids filled their sleeves. Such a scene in such an atmosphere was unique in the Lingnan gardens, which proved a good match for gardens in other places.

With coloring, substantial colors are not what is to be aimed at. Though the gardens in Northern China, with green pines and vermilion

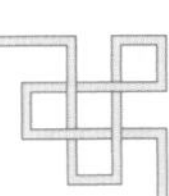

corridors setting out against the white clouds in the blue sky excel in contrasting colors, in the gardens south of the Changjiang River (Jiangnan gardens), the little pavilions giving onto waters and the low white-washed walls may vary in a thousand and one ways. Whiteness is no color, but out of it grow colors. Water in the pond is colorless, yet it is richest in colors. Accordingly, in a Chinese garden scenery should be sought where there is no scenery, sound in soundlessness, and motion in stillness rather than in motion. A pond is like a huge mirror in a garden. That is what we call scenery within scenery, which can only be sought where no scenery is supposed to be found.

It is appropriate to have more deciduous trees in a small garden with an emphasis on spacing so as to produce an effect of openness and spaciousness. However, in a large garden, a suitable number of evergreens should be added to what the garden already has so that the visitors will not feel emptiness in it. This is the principle of compensating for crowdedness by means of sparseness, and emptiness by means of concentration. The deciduous trees can reveal the seasons of the year while the evergreens can withstand the cold of winter. As frigid weather sets in early in Northern China pines and cypresses are usually planted there.

Rocks have no regular shape, but there are certain rules in the setting out of rockwork. These rules refer to the veins and the whole bearing of the rockery and correspond with the principles of painting. Nevertheless, *shi* (a type of verse popular during the Tang dynasty) perished because of its rigid rules and forms; *ci* (a type of verse popular during the Song dynasty) fell into decay because of its strict tonal patterns and rhyme schemes. Yet the excellent lines of *gufeng* (a kind of ancient poetry) of the Han and Wei dynasties and of *xiaoling* (a type of *ci*) of the Northern Song dynasty were never harassed by patterns and rhymes. As a matter of fact, the poems (*shi* and *ci*) composed by pedantic scholars displayed no

intelligence or aesthetic charm. The same is true of garden designing.

With rockeries, unevenness exists in the flat and curves in the straight. The garden maker should have an overall picture in view and start with laying his hands on details. It is easy to build the base part of a rockwork but difficult to finish its top with Huang rocks, and vice versa with Hu rocks (rocks from the region around Tai Lake). A Huang rock structure should be so constructed that visitors will be able to detect a sense of hollowness and flexibility in its vigorousness whereas in setting up a rockery made up of Hu rocks a sense of vigorousness should never be overlooked while hollowness and flexibility are being emphasized. In a word, the drawback of a Huang rock structure is lack of change and that of a Hu rock structure is that it looks fragmentary and scattered. Rock varies in shape and quality, and in veins and lines. What is needed here is a dialectical approach and no hard and fast rules should be applied. It is certainly an arduous task to form a miniature hill made up with Huang rocks which zigzags and is landscaped on all sides or one made of Hu rocks which possesses a natural grace and charm in its various postures.

It is difficult to achieve weightiness and unsophisticatedness in rockery formation, still more so in laying out a hill of primitive simplicity. Likewise, it is most difficult to build forbidding cliffs. In setting out rocks hanging out over the water, rocky slopes, stone stairs and stone steps, as with the little masterpieces by the great painter Ni Yunlin, the points that are liable to be overlooked actually demand our whole attention. Painstaking effort, studied deliberation and a careful appraisal and analysis of the whole scenery are required before the dexterous brushes touch on the canvas lightly and casually as done in portrait painting. Adding three hairs on the cheeks is the finishing touches that give life to the boy's whole mien. Meticulous attention should be paid to points that might easily be neglected. Ming rockeries were characterized by strength and massiveness which always evoke contemplation in visitors. The rockeries of the Tongguang period of the Qing dynasty sought to excel by sophistication but were found to be too delicate, even a bit fragile.

Actually there is no rockwork that excels nature but resorts to simplicity. The beauty of Huang rocks lies in unsophisticatedness which conforms with nature. Any good work of artistic value is invariably integrated with its innate qualities.

The layout of Ming rockeries was very simple. They were composed of stairways, flat terraces, main peaks, caverns and ravines and nothing more, but with a myriad of variations derived from two entirely different types of setting — the open and the closed types. With the former ravines are hewn out of the hills. The grand rockery in the Yu Yuan of Shanghai is a fine example. With the latter the main peak sticks out and the ranges rise one after another distinctly. Hills with the remaining mountain chains and scattered rocks belong to the formulas of the open type. Hence keeping the base of a hill and scattered rocks for the dry rockeries and devising the jutting-out rocks by waters and rocks in the pond or in rapids for the wet ones follow the same concept. Brevity constitutes the soul of Ming landscape paintings whereas Qing paintings were characterized by overelaborateness. It can be seen that both features had their impact on the rockery laying — out of the two dynasties.

The Ming scholar Zhang Dai[1], nicknamed Tao'an, wrote about *Sanfeng* Rocks (rocks on three peaks) in Wang Yuan at Yizheng in his

1. Zhang Dai: 1597-1679, man of letters of the late Ming and early Qing Dynasties.

Notes about Dreams of Tao'an: "I found an abandoned white rock in the garden, ten Chinese feet in height and twenty in breadth. It looked crazy. Yes, 'crazy' is the very word to depict it. And a black rock, eight Chinese feet in breadth and fifteen in height. A very spare rock. And 'spare' is just the word for it." Zhang used "crazy" and "spare" to describe the rocks because he had instilled sentiments into them. And the Qing poet Gong Zizhen[1] used the phrase "pure and ugly" on men, which phrase would be most appropriate when applied to rocks. The Huangla rocks at the newly-set-up viewing points in Guangzhou's gardens are very "obstinate". The word "obstinate" added to "crazy" and "spare" invented by Zhang will make the description perfect.

Rockery formations in a dry garden can be so set as to create a sense of water. Typical examples are the rockeries at the back section of Qiuxia Pu at Jiading, Shanghai, and in front of the Two-Thirds of the Bright Moon Hall at Yangzhou. In spite of the absence of natural waters in the garden, the undulating rockworks contrasted with the sunken ground

1. Gong Zizhen 1792-1841, man of letters and thinker of the Qing Dynasty.

give the visitor the impression of a scene with something like a pond set in it. Thus a sense of water is created. It would be a grave mistake if you want to keep the rock structure in water and try the formulas of a dry rockery, and vice versa, because the base of a dry rockery and the ingress and egress of a wet one are entirely two different matters. Moreover, cliff-paths, projecting rocks and water bends belong to the wet rockery and do not apply to the dry type, whereas the base part of the dry rockery and the scattered rocks are alien to the grace and charm of a wet rockwork. It is plain that the rules for Hu rocks do not work with Huang rocks. Neither do those for Huang rocks work with Hu rocks. In short, a garden designer must observe natural landscapes, study the theories of painting, take nature as his teacher, exert his intelligence and draw inferences about constructing new rockeries from his own experience. Only in this way can he make a success of what he has laid his hands on.

With gardens there are cases of a large garden encircling small gardens and in scenery a large lake encircling small lakes. A masterpiece of the latter is Three Pools Mirroring the Moon in the West lake. The Ming literator Zhong Bojing (1574-1624) wrote in his *Notes about the Plum Blossom Villa*: "Water is everywhere in the garden. There you can find a tall flat terrace, a massive house, a light and void pavilion, a winding corridor, a ferry crossing, perpendicular rocks, singing birds and fragrant flowers, and visitors coming and going — each of which forms an integral part of the garden. Then why should people have a garden of their own? You are in a garden, yet you are not aware of it. Well, if a garden comprises a

number of gardens, you will realize that you are in the garden. This is the way with most people in the world." Here philosophical theories may be drawn into garden designing.

The scenery outside the garden contrasts and echoes well with the scenery inside the garden, forming a wonderful picture. Great skill is revealed in a careful selection of location. The following is also from Zhong's *Notes about the Plum Blossom Villa*.

"Huge volumes of water are drawn from the Suzhou area and the water does not flow freely till it comes to Fuli (Luzhi). No water can be seen a few steps away from the villa, but water is found within it. A concealed hole has been made to lead water into the garden. Opening the door, I take a stroll at an easy pace. I pass Qi Ju Study... and climb the storeyed-building. What I see is not water entirely. Nonetheless, water is where the pavilion strides across, where the corridor leads to, where the bridge is set up, where the rocks, horizontal and vertical, rise from and where the drooping willows and tall bamboos spread over and give shades and coolness to ... As I stare with narrowed eyes into the distance from the storeyed building, an enchanting scene comes into sight — the water is encircled by the corridor and the corridor by the wall. It looks as if a storeyed structure was looming there. Tall and erect grow the trees and plants outside the wall, and so green is the flow of water that visitors' skirts and garments look green in it. It seems that you could scoop up the water and hold it in your arms, yet you cannot reach it. ... Then I get through Xiaoyou Cave and stop for rest in Zhaoshuang Pavilion. At the water's edge the mossy stones keep gnawing at the ripples. Here is what is known as Jingcong Beach. I then make for the Long Corridor, which is found running side by side with a stream. Bamboos grow along both sides of the stream. Here water shares breezes with the bamboos and the two compete for sunlight while the gurgles of the flow and the rustles of the leaves become interwoven in daylight. You can almost feel all this. It is practically impossible to select a place which will be best for viewing the scenery in a hurry, and a corridor has been erected for the purpose." In the garden mentioned in the *Notes* water plays an exceedingly important role. Plans have been made to deal with it: whether it should lie concealed or exposed, whether it should be kept inside or outside

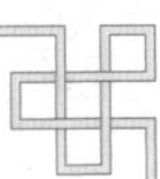

and whether it should have its rises and falls and curves, all depend on circumstances. To make water serve the garden, pavilions, corridors and storeyed-structures should be set around it, because buildings are the only means to bring about the changes in space of both water and land. Hence "all gardens are separated and all waters are curved." Of the corridors built around water now existent, the one in the western section of Zhuozheng Yuan has been profusely praised. And the design of the waterways in the Plum Blossom Villa has some semblance to it. The gardens in Suzhou can be traced back to the same sources.

The venerable Tong Jun (1900-1983), famous contemporary Chinese architect, once remarked that in the Zhuozheng Yuan "the moss-covered paths, the hillocks and ponds that resemble natural landscape and the houses with faded colors give visitors great comfort and pleasure." Slightly dilapidated, with hills and valleys that have a distinct character, the garden retains its natural grace and beauty. It follows that simplicity and unsophisticatedness in the design of a garden is far superior to embellishment and affectation. The grandeur of the Liu Yuan in Suzhou lends that garden the air of a most sumptuously decorated hall — the Seven Treasure Hall. Not a small portion of the hall is to be damaged. A little wear and tear and the garden falls into decay. In recent years renovation of gardens of scenic beauty was either neglected or overdone. Take Zhuozheng Yuan for example. Formerly the revetment of its pond presented a wonderful picture of rock interwoven with earth, but now earth has simply vanished from the scene. The scene is like a man showing off his whole set of gold teeth in the mouth. Another example is the Bayin Ravine in the Jichang Yuan at Wuxi. Deprived of its balance, the ravine has lost its former charm. Is it not clear that utmost discretion and meticulous care should be exercised in carrying out renovations of this kind?

The secret of showing the scenery to advantage lies in "outlining" it. Recently, at the invitation of an organization in Changzhou I went there to hold discussions with them about the layout of the Red Plum Blossom Hall Yuan. My idea is that since the garden has for its name the Red Plum Blossom Hall, red plum blossoms should be its dominant feature. Yet the Plum Nursery would be more appropriate name for a garden of several hectares, planted with plum trees all over. Besides, a landscape garden can hardly be accomplished in a short period of time. I suggest

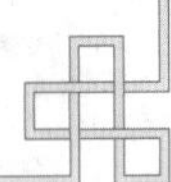

that a long corridor be built across the garden and [illegible] irregularly outside the corridor. Amidst the scatte[illegible] uneven plums, visitors saunter, their garments scented [illegible] of plum blossoms. In this way the visitors will naturally get the idea of red plum blossoms though the garden's actual name is not mentioned. The magnificence of the scenery is brought out by the corridor which "gives contours to" many points of interest in the garden and succeeds in turning each of them into a beautiful picture. This is an instance of what we may call "making few surpass many" and "seeing the large through the small."

It is not so difficult to achieve density as sparseness in a garden; neither is it so difficult to be gorgeous as to be quietly elegant. The central section of Zhuozheng Yuan is a fine embodiment of such qualities as being sparse yet not expansive, quietly elegant yet not shabby. It is fair that Zhuozheng Yuan has enjoyed great fame throughout the land south of the Changjiang (Yangtze) River since the Ming dynasty. It is a pity that these principles are not appreciated in garden restorations.

People in ancient times would give their garden a name when it was completed. The name was not chosen at random but it had its implications. The following is taken from what Yang Zhaolu in 17 century wrote after he had constructed Jin Yuan at Changzhou. "After I fell ill and returned home I bought a piece of waste land, six or seven *mu*, behind the Zhujing Hall. I had been working at it for five years before it began to take the shape of garden. Therefore I called it Jin Yuan (Resembling a Garden)." When I learned of the origin of the name I praised the author for his modesty. Now I recall that the year before last I saw in the Rain Lake Park at Maanshan City a poorly-set-out pavilion, still without a name. I was asked to name it and I put down "Zan Pavilion" (Temporary Pavilion). What was implied was left unsaid, yet everybody had it. The name is an antithesis of such names as "Grand View Garden" and "Ten Thousand Willows Hall".

The Suzhou gardens have had great impact on the stage design and decoration of the traditional Chinese theatre. But natural scenery and stage scenery are different. Today, however, we find architectures in landscape gardens are modelled on stage setting, ingeniously and exquisitely wrought, light and delicate, just like those cleverly and intricately handmade paper models on sale at the City God's Temple in

滄浪亭

Shanghai, or a painting done in blind imitation, which makes a good show of its frivolities and has the ludicrous effect of an ugly woman knitting her brows in imitation of a famous beauty of her times only to make herself uglier.

Carved hollowed-out lattice windows have the effect of "revealing the scenery" and "drawing out the scenery". Scenery in a large garden might as well be revealed but in a small garden it is proper to draw out the scenery and not to reveal it. The "Crabapples in a Spring Flower-bed" in Zhuozheng Yuan is a courtyard, therefore, the carved hollowed-out lattice windows there can draw out the scenery in a large garden. But the Yi Yuan of Suzhou is a small garden, and the two large carved lattice windows inserted in the walls on either side of the garden gate

spoil the whole thing. The windows do not match the garden, and the scenery, exposed, is deprived of its subtle beauty. The garden's new gate having too much solemnity of the imperial court may be compared to an ancestral hall, thus providing a striking example of inappropriateness for Chinese gardens. Another type of mistakes that go against the principles of garden designing is that the new buildings set up in the scenic spots and places of historic interest tend to overshadow the old ones. Many instances can be cited to prove this. As modesty is a virtue, it is hoped that new buildings will be reconciled to their minor roles and will then be appreciated and praised by the public.

"Ponds and halls are changed as people wished; the distinguished scholars' posthumous works are to drift with the east-going current; my eyes brimming with tears, I climb the tall storeyed-building." Those were the lines I wrote in memory of the two venerable old scholars, the late Mr. Liang Sicheng and the late Mr. Liu Dunzhen[1] when I saw the damage that had been done to the gardens as I revisited Yangzhou a few years ago. Those lines were written with deep emotions. While writing *On Chinese Gardens* (*Part Two*), I also feel the urge to say something. And this time I am writing with a different mind.

Translated by Wu Yiyun

1. Liang Sicheng and Liu Dunzhen were both distinguished scholars and renowned specialists in architecture.

Part Three

Restoration

AND

Renovation

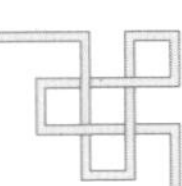

I have already presented the two pieces of *On Chinese Gardens* and since I am deeply in love with the topic, I feel impelled to give expression to some more of my humble sentiments. That has led me now to take my seat before the sunny window of my study, with writing paper spread out before me. What I am going to say may only be a medley of insignificant or even trivial views, but I do hope to arouse some interest in my readers and to be corrected where necessary. With this in mind, I shall call the present piece *On Chinese Gardens* (*Part Three*).

Poet Tao Qian (Yuanming) (365 or 372 or 376-427) in his essay *Notes from the Land of Peach Blossoms* has this to say: "On a carpet of fragrant, luscious green grass were grown peach trees, now in full bloom, their beauty uncontaminated by heterogeneous growths." This charming piece of description can also be looked upon as a criterion which, being an expression of a uniquely good taste, can well be applied to the art of landscape gardening in scenic spots. Along with the two lines: "Gathering chrysanthemums in the shade of the eastern fences, I sank into a leisurely mood and found myself watching the distant hills to the south," they may be looked upon as masterpieces of eternal poetic value. The first two lines illustrate how peach trees can look better in groves, to which distance lends new beauty. With blooming flowers against a backdrop of green, the beauty of the scenery will, so to say, create itself. The two other lines indicate how "borrowing" can be achieved in the landscaping art. Although no explicit reference is made to garden designing, the fundamental principle of the art is all there.

Watching a distant mountain from a fixed point is like focussing one's eye on an album of paintings, while making a tour of a mountain is like unfolding a hand scroll before one's eyes. With one, the emphasis is on giving prominence to certain features of the scenery, with the other it is on the continuity and integration of scenery. With the two different types of viewing, that is, in-position (fixed-point) or in-motion, man responds differently, in terms of emotion and psychology, to what is in view. The deciding factor here is the presence of the self. This is attested to by the following saying: "I can see the intoxicating charm of the blue hills and I expect to be seen in the same light by them." As to how to achieve such an effect, I believe in the use of the poetic form, annotations or inscription. This accounts for the reason why people say that paintings would look vulgar without a proper inscription and that the beauty of scenery would

be obscured if unaided by cliff-side carvings (or carved couplets). This, as I see it, is because art and literature are after all inseparable. "Listlessly the clouds rise out of the distant hills. Tired of winging on, the birds know it's time to return." Here the appeal is not only in the scenery itself, but also in the accompanying sound and motion which is easily evoked. Once I took a short trip to Yangzhou. After disembarking from my small boat, I stayed in Yue Guan (The Moon Temple) on Xiao Jin Shan (Small Jin Hill), intending to enjoy the beauty of the moon with in-motion viewing while taking occasional short rests to do in-position viewing. Meanwhile, the orchids around me were exuding an intoxicating scent, the bamboos

were playing with their shifting shadows, the birds were chirping and the oars of the small boat were making tiny plashes in the stream. While all this was going on, the westering sun was casting its last slanting rays on the window lattices. The fragrance, the shadows, the light and the sounds were all woven together into one harmonious whole. The overall effect in a situation like this is the realization that in stillness one can detect motion while in motion there resides stillness. Here then, in a sense, is the embodiment of the laws of dialectics as manifested in the designing of gardens and in the appreciation of beautiful scenery.

In a garden, some scenic features may be there as a result of deliberate planning. There are, however, also cases where good scenery may have been created mainly by circumstance. This is especially true with small-size private gardens where restricted space may compel the designer to take extraordinary measures, thus saving the situation by turning disadvantage into advantage. Take for instance that part of Liu Yuan in Suzhou which is called Hua Bu Xiao Zhu (Flower Step Court). Here the gateways are all brick-laid, and the path has been sectioned off into long, narrow walkways, creating in the tourists such feelings as are reflected in the lines: "Deep, deep is the courtyard. How deep can it be!"

There are things that properly belonged to the past and there are things of the present. Each category is only amenable to its own criteria which can ill apply to the other. The same is true of things that are foreign in origin and things that are indigenous, which in the present case mean things that are peculiarly Chinese. The past and the present, what is foreign and what is Chinese, each category has evolved into an independent system and it simply would not do to have one take the guise of another. It is fallacious to ignore the functions of the architectural works of a certain past age and the principles guiding their designers and try to interpret the latter's views in completely modern-day terms. Take for instance the makeshift short-cut paths under the eastern walls of Wangshi Yuan in Suzhou. They were designed for the exclusive use of servants and menials who were expected to be as unobtrusive as possible, just as in a big mansion of the past there may have been built what were called "avoidance lanes". These paths form a sharp contrast with the winding covered corridors on the opposite side. There used to be the saying that "Shortcuts offer the greatest convenience but it is the winding routes that exercise the greatest fascination and interest." What I am trying to bring

home here is that one must first make a good study of the history of a garden and familiarize himself with the life-styles of the age before one can say anything convincing about its merits and demerits. In designing a garden, the designer always has in mind a planned tourist route which can be compared to the introduction, elucidation of the theme, transition to another viewpoint and summing up — the four steps in the composition of an essay, or to the foreword, the picture and the postscript of a hand scroll, which form an integrated whole, the order of whose components admits of no wanton reversal. And yet something totally preposterous and unreasonable has now happened. The entrance to Zhuozheng Yuan of Suzhou today happens to be the original eastern side-gate of the garden and that to Wangshi Yuan, believe it or not, is actually the back gate in the north. If I remember correctly, in *The Miscellaneous Notes of Yi Shan*, the writer, in listing those occurrences that ineluctably ruin the effect of good scenery, makes mention of the following unpleasant things: "To shout, in a pine wood, at the pedestrians to make way for an official sedan; to be moved to tears at the sight of flowers; to lay mats on mossgrown ground; to hang out one's washed pants under blossoming

trees, to carry, on a spring outing, a lot of luggage; to hitch to a stalagmite one's horse; to display torches under a full moon; to build a house behind the crest of a hill; to grow vegetables in an orchard; to raise poultry under a latticework for flowering plants" and so on and so forth. Now I would like to make one more addition to this already long enough list, namely, "to throw open the back gate to let in tourists." I would like to know from those in charge of garden management what they think of this. As to the fact that in Suzhou today the four gardens of Canglang Ting, Shizi Lin, Zhuozheng Yuan and Liu Yuan are claimed to be "the four famous gardens of the Song, Yuan, Ming and Qing Dynasty respectively", I can only say that as far as I know both Liu Yuan and Zhuozheng Yuan were built in the Ming Dynasty and underwent renovation during the days of Qing. How come they have now been ascribed to two different dynasties?

This is puzzling. I myself would venture to call Wangshi Yuan a garden good for in-position viewing, Zhuozheng Yuan one for in-motion viewing, Canglang Ting a garden of antiquity and Liu Yuan one of great stateliness and magnificence. Together they may be called "the four famous gardens of Suzhou." Perhaps this will make it easier for the tourists to see each in terms of its own characteristics.

Designing a garden is like composing an essay, allowing a myriad of variations. How can one write a good essay if all one's attention is concentrated on putting together a package of words and phrases, with no idea of the vital importance of the overall conception or of the impact of the piece as a whole? Writing is treasured for its inner force of which style is an expression. Styles may be classified as masculine and virile or feminine and gentle. If this is the way of essay writing, so is it the way of garden designing. A coherent and well-knit piece of work must not be a mere pack of fragmentary and isolated ideas and yet in today's garden design the general practice seems to be to seek excellence by way of building a single pretty pavilion or a single beautiful terraced house. It is indeed true that, without being thoroughly impregnated with traditional

Chinese culture, it is impossible to master the essentia... garden designing.

Architecture in south China is characterized by the prevalence of the shed which features wide-openness while in the north the predominant form is the cabin which is marked by occlusion. The former owes its origin to nest dwellings up in trees and latter to cave dwellings. Open structures in a setting of dense woods and tall bamboo groves, this might be the beginning of primitive gardens. Gardens should have such qualities as spaciousness and airiness, so should architectural works. That is why gardens in north China are, generally speaking, inferior to their counterparts in the south. Good architecture is characterized by a profusion of windows and doors. And occlusion, in whatever form, prevents ventilation and obstructs the view. In the case of rooms for human habitation, there should even be created an air of intimacy. Here are two lines from a poem, "The birds are happy to have found a sanctuary here. For myself, I can only say I too love my humble dwelling." Aren't they an apt description of such a state of mind?

A small-scale garden may be compared to a small-size room with a couple of famous paintings hung on its walls. In other words, it is a place good for doing in-position viewing. A large-scale garden, on the other hand, may be looked upon as an art exhibit boasting a large collection

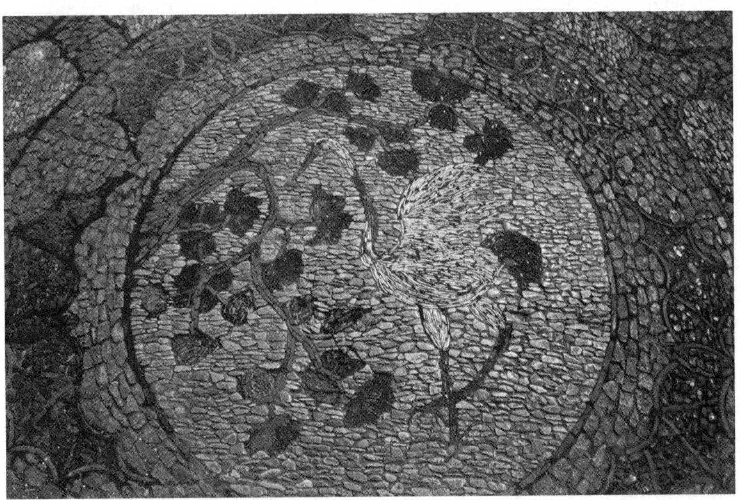

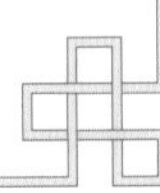

of works. That is to say, it is good for in-motion viewing. This accounts for the reason why gardens of the former type must be rich in implicit values that are capable of sustaining the tourists' interest while those of the latter type must possess foci of special attraction in order not to make the tourists feel them dull and monotonous. Gardens in different ages in history have served different functions. Changes in function have in their turn brought about changes in the way of landscape design and in the way of naming gardens. Thus have come into being two terms of small-scale public garden and large-scale public garden (public as opposed to private). They sounded quite acceptable in pre-liberation days but now their use is rather in doubt. I have questioned the use of the word "public" here and now have been told that in Nantong what was once called the Lang Shan (Wolf Hill) Public Garden has been renamed Beilu Yuan (The Northern Foothills Garden), that the former Chengdong Public Garden of Suzhou is now Dong Yuan (The East Garden) and that the Bianjing Public Garden in Kaifeng is now called Bian Yuan (The Garden of Kaifeng). These gardens seem to have taken the lead. As to gardens in urban areas, in the suburbs, on flat land or at the foot of hills, each type should be designed in line with its special topographical features. They must not follow an identical pattern.

In doing renovation work in ancient gardens, there is often a lack of awareness or understanding of the designer's conception and plan. I would suggest that a distinction be made between "restoration" and "rebuilding". In the case of a garden of great renown, it is imperative that we make a thorough study of all relevant literature and art works so that its old look can be fully restored. If in doing restoration work people insist on doing things their own way, it will only end in rebuilding the place rather than its restoration. We can see an analogy in the re-mounting of ancient paintings. Where certain strokes happen to be missing, the craftsmen should do the best they can to identify and then use the same pigments as the original painter and imitate the latter's techniques so that the picture as a whole would look unblemished. If restoring Ming rockery with the techniques of Ge Yuliang[1] or, working on a piece of landscape painting by Shi Tao[2], with the characteristic strokes of the four Wang's[3], the result would be a completely changed work of art. Wouldn't one feel conscience-stricken at having thus ruined the artistic creations of his

1. Ge Yuliang: 1764-1830, master of garden rockery.
2. Shi Tao: 1641-about 1718, landscape painter.
3. Four Wang: four landscape painters named Wang Shimin, Wang Jian, Wang Hui and Wang Yuanqi in late Ming and early Qing Dynasties.

ancestors? On the other hand, what is involved may only be an ordinary garden at an advanced stage of dilapidation but with remnants of rockery and ponds that can still be utilized. In such a case, it may not be a bad idea if we try to make use of what is left and redesign the garden as we see fit. However, this can only be called "rebuilding".

In China, the birth of "bonsai" as an art was bound up with the history of architecture of the country. In ancient times, residences were made up of a combination of courtyards each of which was surrounded by buildings, corridors or walls. The result is restricted space and insufficient exposure to the sun. Hence in Suzhou and its vicinity, people had a way of decorating their courtyards with miniature rocks and undersize trees which, although exposed to the sky, often were not blessed by the sun. Or it might happen that the morning sun would fleetingly cast its warmth and then quickly be gone. All plant life has a minimum requirement for sun and warmth. If the plants have that, they will be kept alive and people will have something whose sight they can enjoy. Su Dongpo[1] seems to

1. Su Shi: 1036-1101, man of letters and poet of the Song Dynasty.

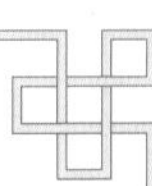

have been most successful in catching the spirit of all this in the following poem:

On and off drips the drizzling rain;
Outside the window, everything is dim and yet more attractive;
The empty courtyard is barely visited by the sun.
How do the plants look? Green and luscious.

It is interesting to note here that even the ordinary things in our life that are born of necessity seek change as a last resort and that it is change that will bring a new lease of life. Another case in point for the law of "survival of the fittest." Nowadays, one is likely to find in a spacious wide-open garden "bonsai" in their hundreds or trees more than ten feet tall planted in pots. People would probably think of these as being impressive in number or size, but sadly out of place. Further, given the fact that the plants are continually exposed to a blazing sun and blustering winds which quickly evaporate what moisture there is, they can not be expected to survive for long. This is an illustrative case of making blind decisions on the strength of inadequate knowledge of the right way of doing potted landscaping.

It is difficult to make a magnificent garden look lightly ornamented. On the other hand, there is often a need for richer colours in a lightly ornamented garden. Ornamentation should be restrained so that a garden will not look gaudy and yet colour is needed to compensate for plainness. The important thing is to be able to create an intensity of effect with simple techniques and present a style of great force with as few touches as possible. As Yan Shu (991-1055), *ci* poet, once

said in the following poem:

Over the pear blossoms in the courtyard is a gentle, watery moon;
On the pond the willow catkins play, astir in breezes light and gentle.

To be beautiful without being gaudy, to be light-toned and yet impregnated with meaning, this is the quality all artists should aim at.

Gardens of the royalty tend to be over-ornamented while private gardens, because of the master's limited means, often betray a touch of sparingness. It is best to be able to keep a good balance between excess and defect without either overdoing or underdoing things. To this end, one should be ready to give up what one may at heart cherish and be unsparing in making additions where necessary. One should keep in mind that the pen he has in hand might weigh a hundred-weight so that every word and every stroke he wants to commit to paper is worth weighing and re-weighing. It is not often that a young maiden from a gentry family can avoid a style which is over-delicate and feminine in her paintings or that Buddhist or Taoist paintings will not betray any traces of monastic simplicity. Virility and gentleness may in fact complement each other. To impersonate a scholar who does not look shabby and pedantic or to play the part of a general who retains the airs of a scholar-gentleman, these are rare achievements. The art of garden designing is governed by the same

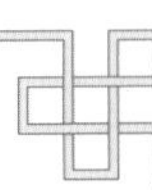

principles as other forms of art. That has led me to assert that Ming gardens reflect the same kind of sensibility and mentality as the literature, fine arts and drama of the age. Only the form assumed is different.

One must first acquire a good taste for appreciating the beauty of a garden before he can learn the art of garden designing. First a good taste and then improved craftsmanship will follow. There is no one who can make recipes without a delicate palate. That is why the man in charge of garden designing must be superior to ordinary practitioners in learning and cultivation. Ji Cheng, when referring to success in building gardens, once said: "The builders may take thirty percent of the credit but seventy percent of the credit must go to the master." Here he is only trying to make people see what an important role the man in overall charge plays without the least intention of insulting or humiliating the workers. Some people today castigate Ji Cheng for remarks like this, which only serves to show their own ignorance of Ji's *Yuan Ye*. Threatening one's opponent in academic discussions with political labels is an outdated practice, at least as I see it.

In understanding the relationship between what is real and what is only imaginary, one needs a proper dialectic perspective. Take the case of Daguan Yuan (The Grand View Garden) in *A Dream of Red Mansions*. Here fiction is perfectly mixed with fact. Call something fictitious and yet it may be based on a prototype the author has seen or even touched. Call something real and yet it may have been enlivened by the author's imagination. That is why the book has such fascination for and appeal to the reader. The same is true of the use of rockery. If it can be made to look like the real thing, it will have a fascinating effect. On the other hand, if a real hill happens to assume the look of a manmade one, it will make the viewers wonder. Sometimes a real human being may look exactly like a created image such as a statue

and sometimes a created image can be made so lifelike as to seem to be breathing and this is when man's curiosity is tickled. In garden designing, what is essential is to make oneself able to "empathize". There is no lack of people who have made garden designing their lifelong career and yet do not have an adequate understanding of this underlying principle. Indeed, the art of garden designing is a most difficult one. In displaying rockery in a garden, the same principle of combining the real and the unreal holds. In appraising and enjoying garden scenery, it is necessary to bring to bear one's full emotional capacity in order to be empathetic and then to be able to personify the objects in view.

A constant topic with relation to art and literature is the artistic conception which is also constantly referred to in garden designing. In

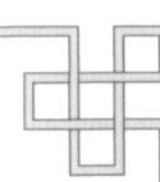

Ren Jian Ci Hua (Notes and Comments on Ci *Poetry in This Our Human World)*, the author Wang Guowei (1877-1927), modern scholar, uses a different term to express the same idea, namely, the world conceptualized in art. With different forms of art, the same term of artistic conception may assume a slightly different form. Hence, with poetry we have what may be called the poetic conception, with *ci* poetry, the *ci* conception and with *qu* (a kind of singing verse), the *qu* conception. "Winding paths lead to a secluded retreat. Hidden behind the flowering plants is the room for meditation" may be looked upon as an exemplification of the poetic conception. For its counterpart in *ci* poetry, the following lines may be cited : "At the end of my dream the big house was found under lock and key. When I sobered up, the curtains and screens were seen deep, deep down." As to *qu* conception, it has found its manifestation in the following lines:

"The vines all seared, the trees all knobby. In the dusky sky ravens are heard to crow."

"An isolated homestead by a small, narrow bridge. Underneath a placid stream is seen to flow."

The artistic conception varies with the setting or the situation. This is also true in the case of its embodiment in the building of gardens. The lyrical and artistic values of a garden depend on the poetic and pictorial conceptions entertained by the designer and embodied in the physical objects on display. We see here once again that the term artistic conception is one of general reference only. In their descriptions of scenery and landscape painting, our ancestors have expressed the following sentiments. The more revealed the physical objects, the more diminished the artistically conceptualized world becomes. The more veiled the objects, the more expanded the conceptualized world in art becomes. "Terrain decides how waters should be made use of. Pine trees should not necessarily be planted in a row." "On all sides the pavilions look out on the waters. Houses are numerous but never obstruct the view of the hills." "The few buildings and terraces are an inexhaustible source of fun. A single winding stream loops itself up and loops everything in." All these were descriptions of beautiful scenery or beautiful paintings by our ancestors when their poetic feelings were aroused, yet they could well be

applied in garden designing. And once applied, what we call the artistic conception will take shape.

In planning the use of rockery and waters in gardens, an integrative rather than a separative approach is needed and there is no set formula to rely on. Hills and waters complement each other, admitting of myriads of combinations. A hill without springs may yet seem to have them and a pond without rockery may still evoke the feeling that what is missing is actually there. A full exploitation of topographical features such as natural highs and lows would give an impression of the presence of hills and waters. This is best exemplified by the area in front of what was once called Gen An (The Mountain Nunnery) of the Gu family in Tieping Xiang (The Iron Bottle Lane) in Suzhou. Garden rockery in south China is often set against a backdrop of white-washed walls, which arrangement may have the effect of enhancing the steep and compact look of the rocks. This probably can account for the origin of paintings on white-washed walls as an art form. Without this backdrop of walls, the rockery would seem like a heap of randomly laid stones. This can also explain the reason why in today's large-scale gardens beautiful rockery is seldom, if ever, seen. Rocks and waters used in garden designing can be compared to the strokes of the painting brush and the dabbings of ink in a Chinese-style landscape painting. A good piece of work is composed of both "bone" and "flesh", that is to say, both framework and details. This accounts for the superb achievements of Shi Tao (Dao Ji) as a painter, whose works are excellent in terms of both framework and details. Banqiao (Zheng Xie) (1693-1765), painter, calligrapher and literator, modelled his work on that of Shi Tao,

but there is an imbalance in his paintings, with, so to say, too much "bone" and too little "flesh", that is to say, overuse of pen strokes and underuse of ink dabbings. This was probably because Banqiao was primarily a calligrapher and only secondarily a painter. If you happen to entrust garden designing to a structural engineer, you will see what artistic and aesthetic effect is lacking.

In laying out buildings at a scenic spot or in a garden, it is necessary to give full consideration to the local conditions. But the main building always faces south on a north—south axis with equal extensions at right angles to east and west horizontally. Such a pattern should be easy to see and yet there are quite a number of people in this field who remain unaware of this. The three temples at Jin Shan, Jiao Shan and Beigu Shan of Zhenjiang are different from each other both in their lay-out and their architectural style. At Jin Shan, the mount itself has become part of the temple, with elevated corridors connecting the buildings. At Jiao Shan, the temple is set in the bosom of the mount with a pattern of distinctly separate courtyards. It is another story at Beigu where the temple is perched on top of the mount, dominating it. Although all of the three look out on the Yangtze River, each gives a full display of its particular view. Jin Shan commands a good long-range prospect, Jiao Shan has a good horizontal view while at Beigu the thing to do is to look down at the surrounding country. Every one of them is oriented towards a superb view and each has a lay-out which has taken into full consideration the best physical features of the place. For all of them, the goal is perfect beauty. How much learning is involved in all this!

Elevation should not be the only criterion for a mountain. What is even more important, in aesthetic terms, is its stratification. For a river or stream, its best feature is not the depth but the sinuosity. The beauty of

a mountain range should be one that takes exploring, its allure lying in the depths of its many retreats. This is characteristic of such south China mountains as Yu Shan of Changshu, Hui Shan of Wuxi, Shangfang Shan of Suzhou and the several hills on the southern outskirts of Zhenjiang. Of the famous mountains of China, Mount Tai is given the first place. This is because, among other things, it is noted both for its peaks and its waters. No one can say that Huang Shan is not beautiful, but, everything considered, there are no torrential water-falls to speak of. If this defect were not redeemed by the presence of perpetually floating mists and clouds, it is unlikely that it could have attained the renown it has today.

With regard to road-building at scenic spots, the roads should be winding rather than straight. If it can be so made that narrow paths and trails will predominate over main roads, then there will be numerous spots of seclusion and the tourists will be able to scatter all over the area. They will look for their own favourite retreats where they can linger around, listening to the tinkle of springs, taking short rests on rocks or lapsing into a contemplative mood and giving play to their poetic impulses. This is reflected in the following lines: "In a mountain, one is always worried that its depths will quickly be explored. In a forest, one always wishes that it could be denser than it is." A mountain is there for the climbing and it is good if the climber can take a short pause at intervals and look

石笋峯
金沙泉

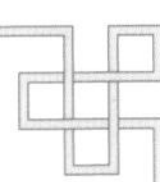

around. This is why in ancient times the general practice was to lay stone steps up a hill. This suited the physical build of the human body that is accustomed to an erect posture. Now stone steps have been replaced by sloping roads which in fact are not only less safe but may even kill the fun of climbing. Even worse, where there should be tourist paths or trails, there are now modern highways with the result that not only has the beauty of the natural gullies and folds been destroyed but swirls of dust are raised everywhere in the mountain. At the same time, the roads are jammed with tourists fighting for their right of way, so to say, against the racing wheels of auto-vehicles. It is indeed not difficult to imagine the congestion of it all and in such circumstances how can one hope to enjoy the pleasures of a mountain trip? Formerly, Yanxia Dong (Cave of Mists and Clouds) on the West Lake was reached by way of narrow trails. Now the place has been made accessible to cars and buses so that it looks no different from the scene before Feilai Feng (Peak That Has Flown in from Nowhere) at Lingyin Temple which is situated on flat land. It has literally become a wideopen area with nothing to obstruct one's view in any direction. Only one might sadly ask whither are the mists and clouds gone? It is said that a plan is now underway to make it possible to organize one-day trips to cover all the scenic peaks around the West Lake. If that should come true, the lake would indeed have "shrunk" a great deal. Only this is contrary to the principle of extending as much as possible the tourist route, and so is not wise at all. To go sight-seeing is a different proposition from to make a journey. Whereas the latter must take into consideration the time factor, the former should be made as slow an affair as possible. Now however

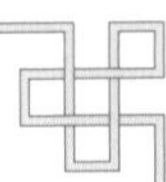

the order seems to have been reversed. Also it is not wise to build spiralling roads up a lone peak as this may leave untapped potential spots of beauty. And the spirals look something like a poisonous snake wound around the neck, cutting up a towering green peak and depriving it of both height and steepness. Witness the two roads that lead up Yuhuang Shan (The Jade Buddha Hill) on the West Lake and Gu Shan (The Drum Hill) in Fuzhou. Fortunately at the latter resort the ill effect is lessened by the presence of folds upon folds of the mountain-side. Hence it is necessary to use the utmost care in designing and building roads in a famous mountain, for once the scenery is spoiled, it is done for for good and all and the spoilers will be blamed eternally by the posterity. As to old access paths into a mountain, they need to be preserved as there will always be tourists who like to go hill-climbing at their own pace. There is another thing we need to give attention to. Mountain springs are often referred to as the eyes of a mountain. Now at several famous scenic areas, the springs have disappeared and are not expected to come to life again. For instance, Baotu Spring in Jinan no longer makes its tinkling music and Jiuxi (Nine Creeks) of Hangzhou is running dry. This is something we really cannot afford to make light of. Opening up a mountain may deface the range and sinking deep wells may end in drawing away the mountain springs. Owing to a lack of coordination between construction work and landscape planning, disastrous consequences have ensued and there is no use repenting. Now look at the Chinese character " 樓 " (pronounced "lou", meaning "many-storied building") and one will see that it is full of holes. The buildings in a garden are expected to be spacious and airy and afford good views on all sides. One ancient poet has these two lines: "At dawn the clouds fly in from the river mouth in the south and play among the painted pillars. At dusk when the bead curtains are rolled up the rain comes in from the western hills." This is his artistic conceptualization of an ideal building. In Chinese, the word 鬆, pronounced as "song" and meaning "pine tree" in English, and the word 鬆 , which is equivalent to "looseness" in English, are not only homophonic but share the same radical too. That is to say, according to the Chinese, pine trees look their best when the branches and twigs are not thickly interwoven and the foliage is not dense. It is often the case that the best effect is seen when opposites such as virility and gentleness can meet and complement each other. For instance, weeping willows look better when

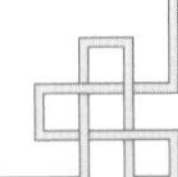

some old and knobby trunks remain whereas bamboos need to exhibit some fresh young shoots. In both cases a good aesthetic effect is achieved by the presence of something from which in ordinary terms no such effect is expected. And yet today all the weeping willows along Bai Di (Bai Juyi's Dyke) on the West Lake have been replaced by young saplings with not a single old trunk still in existence. Hence the dyke no longer looks its old self. How can out-and-out elimination be applied in garden management?

Scenic spots are dotted with tea houses where as a general rule tourists can also find a washroom. The latter's presence has caused many problems to which no easy solution can be found. Personally I would think that it had better be placed with as much concealment as possible. However, all washrooms today are decorated with lattice windows and look rather like "works of art in a garden". Half in jest, I composed the following doggerel: "I want to cry and cry again over the injustice done to lattice works. Who would have thought that they would be part of a structure for a washroom!" (I was of course to blame for the publication back in 1953 of that book entitled *On the Lattice Window*.) One of the functions of this kind of window design is to be revelatory of what is worth seeing inside. But what is there in a washroom for a lattice to reveal? I have seen somewhere a new washroom under construction which has ground-to-ceiling lattice windows. On its left is a stone tablet inscribed with two Chinese characters: Xiang Quan, which means in English: "A Fragrant Spring" while on the right is another which reads: Long Fei Feng Wu, whose English equivalent could be "The dragons are flying and the phoenixes are dancing." At the sight of all this, how can one help breaking into laughter? It is my own humble opinion that at a scenic spot covering an extensive area, it is necessary to have tea houses or tea stands where tourists can slake their thirst. But it is a different story with small-size places of interest, such as Xi Ling Seal-cutting Society on the West Lake or Wangshi Yuan in Suzhou. In places like these, there seems to be no need at all for tea houses which will only take up precious space. Further, what tea houses we have today in big gardens often bear a strong resemblance to guest houses or restaurants. So far I have never seen one that exhibits good taste. My overall impression is that there is a misplacement of priority. At our scenic spots or gardens there seems to be afoot a trend towards more and more commercialization as though the tourists had come mainly to do shopping. If all ancient temples host fairs

and all famous gardens turn into commercial enterprises, then one has every right to lament: "Now that the market place is encroaching on our eastern fences, what disgrace the beautiful yellow chrysanthemums have to bear!" If the Bureau of Park Administration becomes a mere guise for the Bureau of Commerce, then it is only right to say: "What it is doing may be business, but it is not its own business."

The Zhejiang style of putting up rockery attached greater importance to technique than to art. It was noted for its grotto work. Most of the rockery made in this style was in the form of isolated peaks. Its representative works were seen in the Hu's garden on Yuan Bao Street, the Wu's garden in Xueguan Lane and at Wenlan Pavilion of Gu Shan (The Lone Hill), all in Hangzhou. The rockeries at these places were partly redeemed by the presence of waters. In more recent times, there came into fashion the style of setting up on flat ground rockery consisting of a grotto inside and a platform on top. It was simple and unattractive and was characteristic of the work of craftsmen from Dongyang of Zhejiang. They were originally waterworks builders, known as sewage men among folks in Hangzhou, and so had no expertise in the art of rockery work. Nevertheless, these sham artists succeeded in passing themselves off to those who were not knowledgeable. Still later, that is after the 1911 revolution in China, the belief spread that "the more the grottoes, the more inauspicious the place." Fashion changed once again and miniature rockery hills with flower terraces became trendy. In olden times, rockery men from different places joined up with each other into guilds. There was the Suzhou guild, the Ning (Nanjing) guild, the Yang (Yangzhou) guild, the Jinhua guild, and the Shanghai guild, which last was a mixture of the Ning and the Su and was of a more recent date. Beginning from Nan Song (the Southern Song Dynasty 1127-1297), most of the famous rockery craftsmen came from Wuxing and Suzhou. They were variously named in the above-mentioned places. At Wuxing, they were called rockery men; at Suzhou, it was Huayuanzi (flower garden men); and in Zhejiang they had another

name which was rockery master or miniature hill master. In Yangzhou, they were known simply as masons and in Shanghai (formerly the Songjiang Prefecture) as masters of hill-building. The famous father and son team from Yunjian[1] (Songjiang), popularly referred to as the Zhang masons, were highly regarded by the lords and high officials of the day. They took up temporary residence in the capital city and their business was carried on by their descendants who were known as Shan Zi Zhang's (Rockerymen Zhang's). In brief, rockery making in the Tai Hu (The Tai Lake) region had developed its own distinctive style which was different from that of the Ning and the Yang guilds which was otherwise known as the Northern Jiangsu style. All of these guilds and the craftsmen from

1. Yunjian: name of a place, today's Songjiang County of Shanghai.

eastern Zhejiang competed with each other for business. Of course, the rockery men were not equally competent, with good ones as well as bad ones. The mediocre ones looked upon rocks as mere building materials and believed that their whole concern was to put one upon another. They had no idea that a good craftsman needed to be knowledgeable and selective about rocks and had no eye for the fine grains of stones. All that they did was to set themselves to finish a grotto in five days or a rockery hill in ten, and all that they knew was to take a real peak as their model and then to scale down the original. This was a reflection of their ignorance of the proper relationship between what is real and what is unreal. If a question of art should be reduced to a mere matter of proportion, it cannot be called a serious attitude. In the light of this, I need to emphasize once again that rockery work is a real art.

In appraising or dating rockery work, what should one do in order to tell an original piece from a restored piece? I think the way to do it is to look closely at the base part of the rockery or the bottom of a grotto, the reason being that the lower part is less vulnerable to the wear and tear of time, and consequently is easily distinguished from the restored part. The

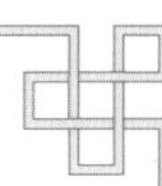

next thing to do is to look carefully at the seams of mortar and the grains of the rocks used. If this is done, one will gradually come to some kind of a conclusion. This is because the seams were differently dated and the mortar used was necessarily made up of different ingredients. Evidence can also be gathered from the cement coating on the rocks and the marks and scars left by axes and chisels. At Liu Yuan in Suzhou, the renovation work done by the Lius during the reign of Emperor Jiaqing of the Qing Dynasty is easily identifiable by virtue of the fact that rocks from Tai Hu had been used on top of the original Huang rocks. Furthermore, rockery of an earlier date was characterized by a very compact structure, with the component parts tightly interlocked with each other. The trick was to achieve a good balance by making the rocks support and nuzzle against one another. With rockery of this kind, once the dismantling was set in motion, it was likely that one would be faced with a heap of loose stones which made restoration of the original impossible. A good piece of remade rockery must have a well-integrated, natural look, with the component parts looking just in place. It should be done in line with aesthetic principles, appearing in natural perspective and in good proportion. Looking closely at the component parts, then at the piece as a whole and weighing all the evidence from all possible angles, this will lead one to the right conclusion.

People today like to talk about the attractions of Yu Yuan in Shanghai but little reference is made to the Pan's mansion which, well known in the Ming Dynasty, was situated only a short distance from Yu Yuan, in the lane next but one to the east of the garden, near where An Ren Street and Wu Tong Road are today (formerly known as An Ren Li). According to Ye Mengzhu in his *Yue Shi Pian* (*Notes on My Experiences in the World*), "No other mansion in Shanghai is equal to it in size. In front is a tall carved screen wall standing guard over the approach to the mansion which is stately and covers an extensive area. Inside there are rows upon rows of spacious buildings with halls and corridors, which make the mansion look the equal of any other lord's home. The buildings at the rear are made of the timber of *Nan* trees. The floors on the upper stories are paved all over with bricks so that walking on them is no different from walking on the flat ground floor. The rooms are all decorated with red lacquer and gold, with delicate wood carvings which exhibit a superb craftsmanship." It seems to me fitting to look upon the above description of the mansion as collateral evidence of the dimensions of Yu Yuan in those days. To our

eternal regret, not even a single trace of this once magnificent mansion is still in evidence.

Yun Shouping[1] (Nantian), a famous painter of the early Qing Dynasty, in volume 12 of his *A Collection of Notes of Ou Xiang Guan* (*House of Fragrance of Wenzhou*), says: "In August of the year *Renxu* (1682), I was invited to stay at Zhuozheng Yuan in Suzhou. It was a time of continual autumnal rains which fell on the woods and made everything so crisp and refreshing. For a time I sat alone in Nan Xuan (The Southern Hall), looking across the waters at the tall and steep rockery on Heng Gang (The Transverse Ridge) which overlooked a clear and lucid pond below.

1. Yun Shouping: 1633-1690, painter of the Qing Dynasty.

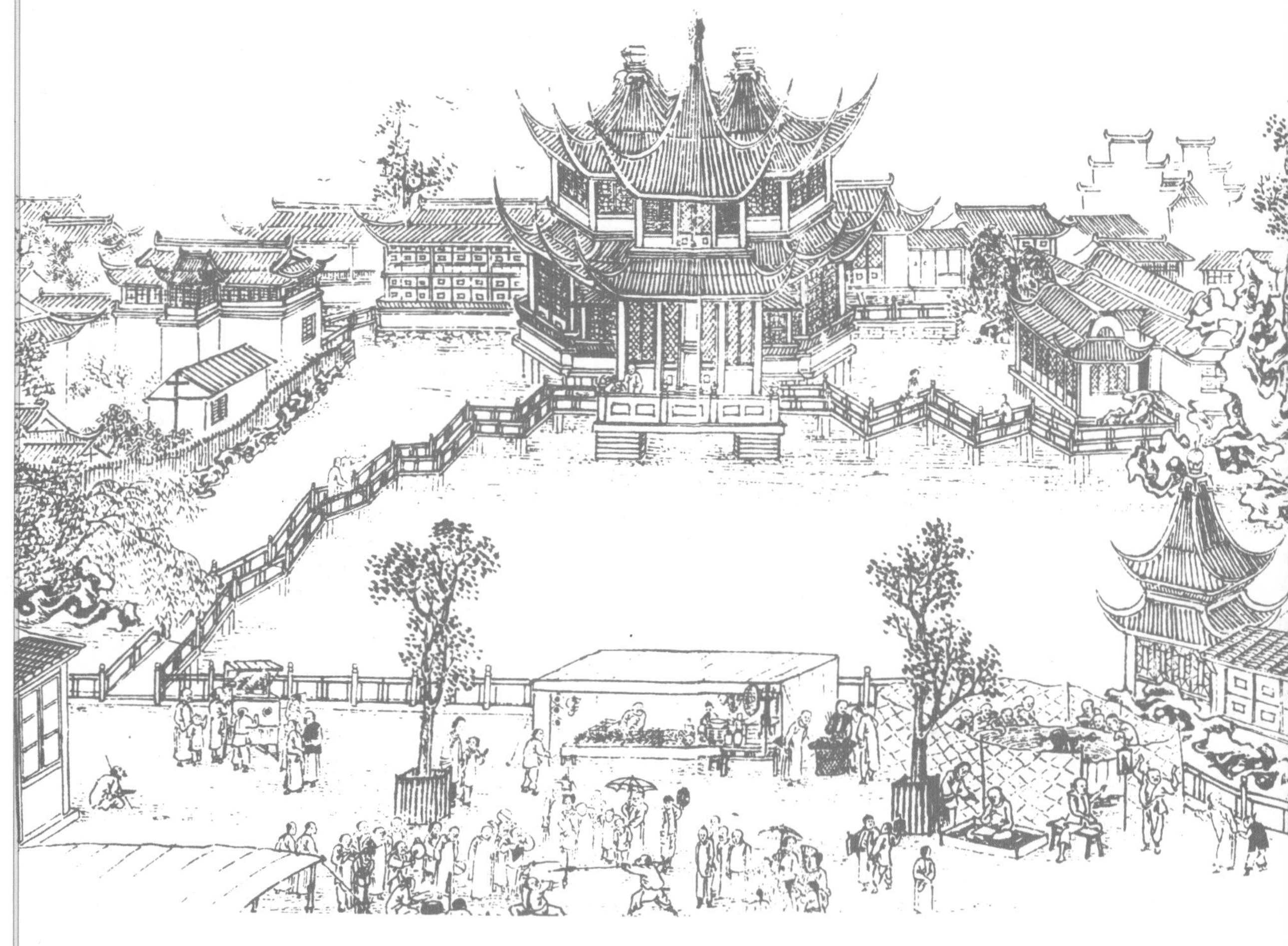

Winding flag-stone paths led up the ridge on which were grown a great many Chinese scholar trees, tamarisks, willows, junipers and cypresses with their intertwined boughs and branches protruding from the dense woods. Along the banks of the pond were planted hibiscus trees with their pleasant mixture of red and green. Looking down at the pond, one could see crystal clear waters with swimming fish which looked almost within easy reach. At the sight of this, one would feel as if he were leisurely enjoying himself in the middle of a vast expanse of waters. Leaving Nan Xuan, I strolled past Yan Xue Ting (The Pretty Snow Pavilion) and made my way north across Hong Qiao (The Red Bridge) onto the flag-stone path on Heng Gang. At the end of the hill, there was a dyke which led to a small mound that was covered with a dense growth of trees. Overlooking the pond was Zhan Hua Lou (Tower of Profound Beauty) which stood face to face with the covered corridors on the opposite bank. It was here that the best scenery of the garden lay." *Renxu* was the twenty-first year of Emperor Kangxi in the Qing Dynasty (1682) when the painter (who lived from 1633 to 1690) was fifty years old. From this detailed account we can make a few guesses. Nan Xuan should be today's Yi Yu Xuan (Hall of the Leaning Jade) and Yan Xue Ting, today's He Feng Si Mian Ting (The Pavilion Where One Enjoys the Fragrance of Lotus from All Four Sides). Hong Qiao must be Qu Qiao (the Serpentine Bridge). Judging by its location Zhan Hua Lou is the site of Jian Shan Lou (The Mountain-viewing Tower) and the covered corridors across the pond seem to be where Liu Yin Lu Qu (The Winding Paths in Willow Shade) is today. This is the scenery of a garden as depicted by a painter. If people doing restoration work could so conceptualize as to get a full understanding of the original conception, they must be highly competent craftsmen. Yet the pity is that, as one poet has lamented, "Few is the number that can fully appreciate such a beautiful song" and we cannot help but sigh over all this. It is not easy to keep a garden in good repair. It is even less so to renovate it. It is often the case that it is better to leave a garden as it is, for once the renovation begins, the whole project will end in a shocking mess. This makes me think that I need to bring this piece to a close on an emphatic note, emphatic in the sense that I would like to reaffirm the importance of studying the history of gardens. Many years ago, one of my respected elders Mr. Ye Gongchuo (1881-1968), a distinguished reformer and calligrapher, wrote me a couplet as a gift. This couplet is composed of the four titles of four books on ancient gardens and historic relics, by which Mr. Ye Gongchuo sought to encourage me in my "gardenphilic" pursuits. The couplet reads as follows:

The famous gardens of Luoyang, and the painted boats of Yangzhou.
Old stories of Wu Lin (Hangzhou), and anecdotes of Beijing.

In the light of what our ancestors have done, perhaps what I am writing now, all things considered, will not be wholly in vain.

Translated by Sun Li

Part Four

The Natural AND the Cultivated

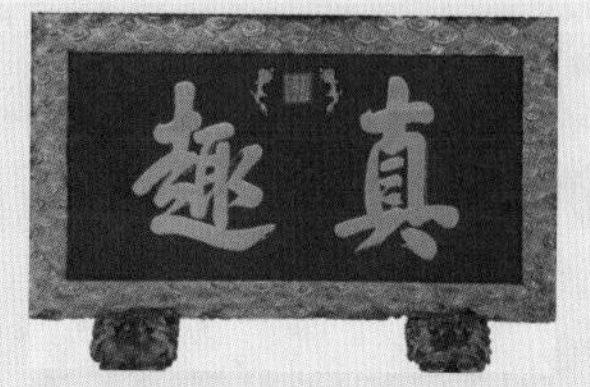
真趣

In my one year's rove, I came across quite a number of scenic spots, and my feelings changed with the change of sights and some humble opinions began to form. I would like to dwell upon them a little with the hope that my readers may judge and exploit them according to their respective views and needs. My opinions are only those of a pedagogue and may not help much in the practical work of garden construction. I state them herein only to evoke discussion. Being a continuation of the previous three essays, the present one is entitled *Part Four*.

In planning gardens, the designer ought to proceed from a conception peculiarly his own and work out the layout of a garden adroitly without the slightest deviation from his original conception. A garden successfully built in this manner will be highly prized whereas a failure will surely induce criticisms. Success or failure, a garden which fails to embody the designer's personality is one devoid of life.

Rivers and lakes serve to set off a terrain of dry land. Therefore, in places where there is little water, ample attention should be given to its preservation; and in districts where water is more than abundant, its drainage becomes a must. Rivers and lakes often highlight the landscape and can be utilized to improve the environment and the climate. In regions criss-crossed with water-courses, lotus and water-chestnuts can be grown in ponds and brooks; bamboo weirs can be erected to catch crabs; and fishing villages can be set up to boost fresh-water fishery. That will help increase people's income without reducing the area of cultivated land. On top of that, the entire region will then be dotted with lovely sights. Wang Shizhen (1634-1711), a poet of the Qing Dynasty, once wrote the following poem:

The ribbon-like stream meanders smoothly
Through nearby fields criss-crossed with willowy paths.
Adjacent to the stream is a fishing village,
Where ponds are overgrown with water-chestnuts.
The view is even more enchanting
When the sunrays are slant and the evening breeze subsides.
Half the stream becomes purple with trees' reflections,

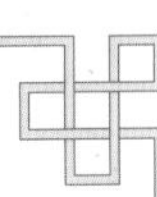

And fishermen start hawking perch.

The scene of natural beauty depicted here is most charming.

In old cities, drooping willows were planted on both sides of the streets. And thick growths of birch-leaf pear trees stretched for miles along the riverside. The crenelations, in their irregularities, appeared vaguely when one looked from afar. The view was a harmonious combination of architectural marvel and natural beauty. Wang Shizhen wrote a verse line: "A verdure of willows, that's the city wall of Yangzhou." Alas, such ancient city walls have now been pulled down and the view is lost forever. The characteristic features of a city consist primarily in its topographic features, and its flora gives the place its distinctive beauty. Chengdu is called the City of Hibiscus Trees and Fuzhou is called the City of Banyans because both cities impress the visitor with their respective flora.

Discussing the art of painting, Yun Shouping said: "When one uses blue and green, special care should be taken to bring out the shades. With these two colours, it's easy to produce dark shades, but difficult to produce light shades. If one thinks it easy to produce light shades, he will find it all the more difficult to produce dark shades." Garden construction follows the same principles, namely, the principles of achieving vagueness in what is substantial and achieving substance in what is vague; of achieving lightness without suggesting flimsiness and achieving stateliness without appearing monstrously heavy. When these principles are followed, in a garden so constructed natural charm will not be lost. Nowadays, people engaged in building gardens in scenic spots often commit follies of wantonly devastating hills and mountains on the one hand and of throwing up artificial rockeries without an apparent overall plan on the other. In their hands, limpid streams are blocked up to give way to man-

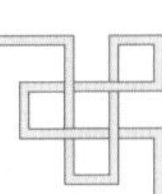

made fountains. They are double sinners. They discard what is natural and indulge in cheap artificialities. They tamper with springs and rocks at will as if a garden without a fountain could never become famous. In an account of the Cork-Tree Mountain Garden in Mount Longmian (literally, Mt. Dragon Asleep), Tongcheng County, Qian Chengzhi[1] remarked: "The Wu[2] people are particularly fond of building rockeries and boasting about them. They laughingly dismiss the gardens and pavilions in my native place as being too shabby. My reply is: 'With all the hills, streams and lakes in my native place, why should we develop an infatuation with artificial ones? We aim at preserving nature. Therefore, our gardens and pavilions are simple in style. Aren't they better than the Wu people's artificial ones?'" Depicting the Garden itself, Qian Chengzhi went on: "The different parts are well arranged without one copying the other with the result that each and every one is a sample of perfection. What is more, there are hills and streams to make the whole place look natural." This remark is excellent in that it brings into sharp focus the word "natural".

The beauty of mountains and forests resides in its naturalness. And by naturalness is meant sticking to whatever is true and real. Buildings are different from gardens in that the former serves to "set off scenery". The relationship between the buildings and their gardens is similar to that between the flowery designs and the brocade. The designs add beauty to the brocade, but they should never be so showy as to blot out the brocade itself. Guest houses are built to provide passengers with a place for a short stay or a pleasant rest. Therefore, the designer should focus on finding a very quiet locale where tourists can ramble about and enjoy pleasant sights. The space within and without the guest house should be made into a coherent entity so as to achieve a kind of expansive harmony. Sojourning here, the tourist, whether bathed in the morning glow or the falling dusk, can visualize a vast landscape while actually being in a limited space. Contrary to this, some guest houses are built on top of a mountain, where tourists reside amidst the jarring horns of motor vehicles climbing up the winding highways. Even birds are frightened away. Peeping downwards, the tourist sees human beings the size of beans and houses shrunk to mere specks. Such small objects are unsightly when set against a vast background. So, metropolitan touches added to a motif of wilderness can only become ridiculously incongruous. As a result, the view is spoilt and the tourists feel disappointed. Leveled

1. Qian Chengzhi: 1612-1693, man of letters of the late Ming and early Qing Dynasties.
2. Wu: today's Suzhou.

hillocks and ravines where high buildings loom and sprawl have almost become a staple sight at tourist resorts. Moreover, I hear that attempts have been made to remove the abodes of mountain folk. What a deplorable mistake not to realize that the scattered dwellings are in fact lovely sights and a component part of the scenic spot. In classical Chinese paintings, we often see landscapes of this pattern. When staying in Switzerland as a guest, I visited some mountain villas in Geneva. They were so clean and tidy that a visitor would cherish a lingering memory of them. It is my belief that buildings in scenic spots had better be so sited that they are half hidden from the view instead of being fully exposed to it, that they are scattered rather than clustered together, and that they, as reasonably low structures, bestrew hillsides rather than stand conspicuously atop as architectural monstrosities. The buildings should be varied in style and display a charming plainness. Their location should be made compatible with the surroundings by skillfully exploiting the advantages of the environment. Guest houses should be made to resemble ordinary dwellings, containing winding corridors

and small courtyards, which are shady with an abundance of foliage and enclosed by whitewashed walls. Such a guest house will be most pleasant to stay at. A guest may repose here alone. He may also invite friends to stay with him. Sojourning here, the guest can enjoy both the comforts of a city residence and the beauty of the wilderness. In his *Notes about Dreams of Tao'an*, Zhang Dai recorded what he saw in Fanchangbai Yuan (i.e., Gaoyi Yuan on Tianping Hill, Suzhou): "A long embankment lined with willows and peach trees encircles the lake, across which creeps a zigzag bridge leading to the garden. Going through the gate of the garden, which is deliberately made low and small, one sees a long corridor as well as some walls shielding the scene behind. The long corridor leads to the foot of a hill, where there are painted houses and bowers with curtained windows. Those buildings are so hidden from the view that they give one a sense of privacy." Another writer Mao Dake[1] in his *Addendum to the History of the Ming Dynasty*, wrote

1. Mao Dake: 1623-1713, Confucian and man of letters of the Qing Dynasty.

some biographical sketches of a certain imperial concubine who was much favoured by Emperor Chongzhen. That imperial concubine was from Yangzhou. She "so disliked the huge dimensions of the palace, the colossus of the flag poles and the immense height of the palace walls that she felt ill at ease at her own abode. Consequently, she moved to a secluded compound where the houses had low thresholds and curving balustrades. Furthermore, she had the new residence screened off from the rest of the palace and furnished it with domestic articles brought in from Yangzhou." These two quotations may serve to prove that my remarks concerning the building of guest houses at scenic spots are not fallacious.

It is obvious that when partitioned into separate quarters, gardens as well as buildings will assume depth with a lot of recesses; otherwise, they tend to look shallow. All such things as rockeries, corridors, bridges, walls, screens, curtains, partition boards, bookshelves and antique shelves have the function to divide. In old times, some bedrooms were furnished with canopies, bed curtains and muslin screens for the same purpose. Similarly, in Japanese houses small bedrooms with mattresses on the floor are divided with screens or paper partitions. Today, guest houses and restaurants by the West Lake are mostly as colossal as palaces. The Louwailou Restaurant on the Lone Hill, a recent construction, is even weightier than the Hall of Clouds in the Summer Palace. That restaurant might as well be renamed the Hall of Supreme Harmony[1] because that would more adequately embody its massiveness. However, even the Hall of Supreme Harmony itself has got screens and columns as partitions whereas the grand dining hall in the Louwailou Restaurant is as spacious as a huge gymnasium. At scenic spots, hills are often cut into to put up dining halls as if barracks were being built there. Preservation of scenery is simply out of the question. What a waste of money and manpower this practice incurs! Ancient gardens had small parlours in the east and west wings. There was never any grand hall. Now we have large guest houses, large dining halls, large frescoes, large potted landscapes and large vases. It seems as if whatever is large is good. What a fallacy!

It is more than a year now since I last visited Suzhou. And I am still frequently dreaming of its famous gardens and historic sites. Recently I received a letter from my friend Mr. Wang Xiye. The letter said: "A potted-landscape garden is being constructed on the ruins of the Eastern

1. Hall of Supreme Harmony: one of the great audience halls in the Imperial Palace.

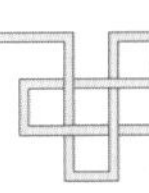

Hill Temple at the eastern foot of Huqiu Hill. The enormity of this new project defies comparison. The Eastern Hill Temple was the memorial temple of Wang Xun[1], who was short of stature and once worked as first secretary to a vice prime minister. Because of this, people of later generations jokingly gave him the nickname "Short Secretary"; and accordingly, the temple was called the Short Secretary Temple. Wang Wan[2] of the Qing Dynasty wrote the following verse in memory of him:

Situated on the long bar,
Was his residence — a garden adjacent to the lucid waters;
Erected on the green hillside,
Is the abode of his soul — the Short Secretary Temple.

Another poet Chen Pengnian(1663-1723) wrote: "Again, the spring breeze sweeps over Daosheng's stones[3]; And the Short Secretary Temple is tinged with the evening glow." These lines have been passed down from generation to generation because they not only convey the poets' profound feelings for the deceased but also display as much beauty as a landscape painting. Today, at the site of that temple, a huge rockery is being constructed with piles of yellow rocks. Consequently, great harm is done to the natural charm of the environment. Though merely a hillock, Hu Qiu is able to vie with the world's famous mountains for beauty. Being half concealed behind a temple, the small hillock seems quite imposing and its Sword Pond, shallow as it is, seems quite deep with a tall cliff on one of its sides. The couplets and poems written by

1. Wang Xun: famous official of the Eastern Jin Dynasty, once first secretary to Vice Prime Minister Xi Chao.
2. Wang Wan: 1624-1691, essayist of the early Qing Dynasty.
3. Daosheng's stones: Daosheng was a learned Buddhist monk of the Eastern Jin Dynasty. He preached on Hu Qiu to stones which nodded with understanding. The stones were therefore called Daosheng's stones.

generations of celebrities in praise of Hu Qiu have lent it an extra charm. Today, a rockery is being piled up in front of the hillock. That certainly amounts to much ado about nothing. I think the designer has made a fool of himself by pretending to be clever. If you can see what is happening here, you will surely wring your hands in great disappointment." What Mr. Wang said here coincides with my views. I'm afraid the man in charge of the project failed to collect the necessary documents and is consequently ignorant of the history of the historic sites. And what's more, he is most likely infatuated with the fallacy that whatever is large is good.

The overall layout of a scenic spot should be so worked out that it may create an agreeable climate as well as an attractive scenery. However, as often as not beautiful sights are created at the expense of the local climate. When I visited the West Lake in July, I was invited by the Garden Administration Bureau to tour the Golden Sand Bay. I went to the Bay at dusk when the lingering heat of early summer was still somewhat oppressive. I roamed into the woods on the Bay and was surprised to find the sweltering summer heat gone. In its place was a cool breeze, a murmuring brook and graceful bamboos. The place was almost as good as a fairyland. Across the West Lake from the Bay, the Southern Hill partially veiled in a thin mist looked green with a dark hue. The whole view was like a wash painting done with exceedingly light brush strokes. Amidst such fascinating surroundings, I did feel that "I could laugh at the intruding southerly wind and even Xi Shi[1] dancing in a rainbow-like costume couldn't be half as enchanting." Though I had grown up at my parents' waterside homestead, I had never experienced such pleasure as I enjoyed there and then. Keeping this coolness unaffected by the heat wave which prevails outside the Bay is actually the goal set down in the original plan for this scenic spot. Once this cool and sweet environment is spoilt, it would be utterly worthless to build a great number of bowers and pavilions there. For this

1. Xi Shi: famous Chinese beauty of the Spring and Autumn Period(770-476 B.C.).

kind of planning fails to abide by the principles governing garden construction. The Golden Sand Bay is situated at the water's edge. Its buildings and bridges are appropriately close to the water surface and their reflections are visible from all angles. The fresh breeze arising from its luxuriant bamboo groves makes the air pleasantly cool. The blue sky above the swaying bamboo tops and the fragrant wafts over the lotus ponds add much to its natural charm. "It's difficult to adorn hills and riversides with thatched pavilions and small bowers. Only a gifted designer will be equal to such a task." If the Golden Sand Bay is strewn with summer houses and bamboo bowers, the place will be as attractive as Xi Shi quietly rouged. I sincerely wish that this summer resort may be well kept so that in my old age I shall be able to come here from time to time to seek leisure and quietude.

Tongli Town in Wujiang County is a very famous scenic spot south of the Changjiang River. The town is surrounded by rivers and almost all the houses in it face each other across waterways, which function as lanes and streets. In face, the whole town with all its gardens is set against waters. Of the gardens south of the Changjiang River, the Garden of Withdrawal for Contemplation has a style all its own and is typical of waterfront gardens. All its rockeries, pavilions, halls, corridors and verandas are built close to the water surface with the result that the whole garden seems to be floating on the water. The view here is different from that of the Wangshi Yuan in Suzhou. The Recluse Garden is close upon the water surface while Wangshi Yuan is adjacent to the waters. By "adjacent to the waters", I mean that the rockeries and buildings, though erected on the waterside, overlook the waters some distance away. Therefore, a garden adjacent to the waters and one close upon the water surface are quite different in style. Though both make appropriate use of the waters,

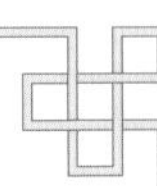

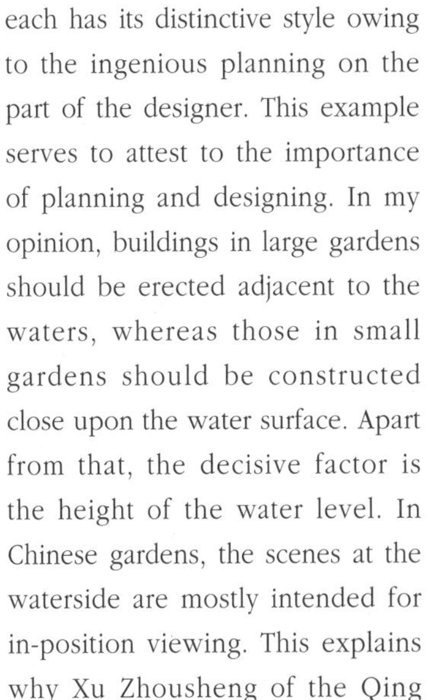

each has its distinctive style owing to the ingenious planning on the part of the designer. This example serves to attest to the importance of planning and designing. In my opinion, buildings in large gardens should be erected adjacent to the waters, whereas those in small gardens should be constructed close upon the water surface. Apart from that, the decisive factor is the height of the water level. In Chinese gardens, the scenes at the waterside are mostly intended for in-position viewing. This explains why Xu Zhousheng of the Qing Dynasty named his garden in Hangzhou "Abode for Contemplating Still Waters". This name embodies the idea of "comprehending movement in quietude", a dialectical conception originating in classical Chinese philosophy.

We all know that the shoreline shapes the water-course, that dykes divide the water surface, that flowers attract butterflies and that mountain rocks invite mists. Therefore, when made best use of, the environment can be rendered exceedingly appealing to the aesthetic sense. Skillful arrangement can add much to the beauty of hills and waters. In small and medium sized cities where there are hills, rivers or lakes to resort to, the miraculous design is one which gives the city an aspect of its own by turning the hills and waters into beautiful gardens.

The Pearl Spring in Jinan enjoys a nation-wide fame for its pearl-like bubbles arising in the transparent spring. One day I visited the Pearl Spring at dawn, when the whole place was just beginning to be tinted. The air was moist with dews. The crispness and serenity of the atmosphere

were simply thrilling. But alas, when I revisited it, the view had been vastly changed. The huge rockeries piled up with brown rocks were ugly and forbidding. The towering buildings around the Spring were oppressive. In *Watching Mount Tai from Afar*, Du Fu wrote:

I am determined to reach the summit;
Viewed from it all surrounding mountains will look dwarfed.

It's surprising that these lines should have found expression at the Pearl Spring! The hillock here looks dwarfed with huge buildings towering on its top. The small brooks here are spanned with immense bridges. Motor vehicles speeding along the hillside highway keep sending up clouds of dust. This sort of planning with imposing structures in a limited space conforms neither to the traditional nor to the modern style; it is neither Chinese nor western, and consequently, neither fish, flesh, nor fowl. Can we afford to be unscrupulous in designing gardens?

Entirely different from the Pearl Spring is the Shihu[1] Garden in the city of Weifang in Shandong Province. The garden is so named because it is fairly small. In this garden there is a pond, which is surrounded with long corridors. Its waterside bowers seem to be floating on the ripples. The scenes here are meticulously arranged to render the place exquisitely graceful. Inspired by its elegance, I wrote the following verse:

Though aged, I am still in high spirits
And love to tour rivers and lakes;
At the sight of fine gardens and charming scenes
I cannot help making comments.

1. Shihu: "Shi" in Chinese means "ten" while "hu" means "tablet", usually made of ivory, held by Chinese feudal officials when received in audience by the emperor. So "shihu", meaning "ten tablets", denotes a length of approximately ten feet, each tablet being about one foot long. Therefore, Shihu Garden means a garden covering a very small area.

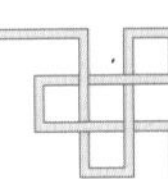

Small as the Shihu Garden's bowers and pavilions,
The feelings they inspire in me are boundless.
I linger amidst the waterside rocks and boulders,
And my heart is filled with tender affections.

Of all the small gardens in North China, the Shihu Garden is certainly the best in fully revealing the beauty of waters and rocks.

The mountain path leading to the summit of Mount Tai has eighteen hairpin bends, each forming a scene peculiar to itself. The view keeps changing with the ascent of the visitor and the spectacle is tremendously magnificent. Looking down from the South Heavenly Gate, the visitor will be thrilled to see unfolded before him a majestic view: lying prostrate at his feet are range after range of green mountains, which extend for over a thousand miles in all directions. Since ancient times, countless kings and emperors have ascended the summit to pay tribute to Providence. With imperial flags on the summit, all the surrounding mountains would seem to be looking up in awe. If a visitor rides in a cable-car, his ascent and descent will be speedy. But on the other hand he won't be able to see the sights. As a matter of fact he will be transported from one place to another like a commodity. What's more, the cable-car is nothing less than a blot on the landscape. I'm afraid that the use of the cable-car only indicates that the visitor doesn't know what mounting the "eighteen hairpin bends" and paying homage to the Jade Emperor Summit means. In fact, to conquer Mount Tai is to experience the grand sensation of seeing the world lying at one's feet. Talking about the difference between travelling and sight-seeing, I once said that travellers would like to move fast while sight-seers wouldn't like the idea of being hurried along. If we fail to realize this, we won't be able to do justice to the famous mountains. I'm not saying that cable-cars should be discarded. What I want to make clear is that cable-cars may facilitate fast travelling, but they can't possibly facilitate sight-seeing.

We mustn't encircle famous mountains with high buildings or factories because they tend to cut the enclosed area off from the entire mountain range. Yet, almost everywhere can we see examples of this sort of bad planning. Recently I visited the Swallow Rock and the Evening Glow Temple in Nanjing. At these two places, there is nothing to suggest any beautiful scene until a visitor reaches the scenic spot itself. He feels as if he were listening to an opera without an overture where the protagonist keeps chanting alone. The view is not panoramic. Take the Swallow Rock. Only the side facing the Changjiang River still retains some of its charm. All the other sides are shrouded in clouds of black smoke, which keep rolling along as fiercely as the torrential Changjiang River. Sitting on the Swallow Rock, I knocked up the following doggerel as a sort of mockery:

Swallow, oh swallow,
Why don't you fly away?
If you keep perching here,
Your doom will be near.

I had felt obliged to visit this scenic spot of the past, but now I wouldn't dare to visit it a second time. Though we mustn't put up

tall buildings or factories at the foot of a hill, yet low structures are indispensable. When dotted with rows of low structures, the landscape will assume some measure of depth and quietude. This is the method of making a mountain look distant by hiding its bottom away.

In recent years, the contradictions between the preservation of scenic spots and the development of industry and mining have become more and more conspicuous. Frequently people act as ridiculously as one who kills a hen to get her egg. For example, Mufu Hill in Nanjing is being opened up for its mineral deposits. And the Evening Glow Hill is being turned into a silver mine. Such a practice is not unlike replacing a factory that doesn't emit smoke with one that does; nor is it unlike tapping exhaustible resources by destroying inexhaustible resources. The result will be the destruction of both. We should look at things from a

long-term point of view and weigh gains and losses properly. I sincerely hope that those in charge will not regard this problem lightly. At historic sites, the focus should be on what is historic, and anything inharmonious must be kept off. The TV towers built on the North Peak in Hangzhou and on the Drum-Tower in Nanjing are shocking examples. In this connection, I would like to make it clear that at scenic spots, scenery should be given first priority while in places of historic interest first priority should be given to things historic. Nothing else is allowed to take precedence over them. Otherwise, the beauty of the country's landscape will be spoilt and our rich cultural heritage destroyed.

While at his post as governor of Hangzhou Prefecture, Bai Juyi[1] of the Tang Dynasty organized the dredging of the West Lake and the building of the White Sand Dyke. He never went so far as to have tideland enclosed for cultivation. Su Shi of the Song Dynasty organized projects of the same kind. Ruan Yuan[2] of the Qing Dynasty carried on the work initiated by the two predecessors. For hundreds of years, people have been singing praises of their virtue and even today the memorial temples of Bai Juyi and Su Shi are still standing on the southern slope of the Lone Hill. Yu Dafu[3] paid tribute to them in the following line:

The willow-lined dyke is still named Su.

To make a city prosperous, it's important to exploit its advantages.

1. Bai Juyi: 772-846, famous poet of the Tang Dynasty.
2. Ruan Yuan: 1764-1849, noted scholar of the Qing Dynasty.
3. Yu Dafu: 1896-1945, modern novelist and essayist.

The West Lake makes up the lifeline of Hangzhou. Its ruin would mean Hangzhou's decline. It is precisely because of the West Lake that the government has decided to build the city into a tourist resort. In working out its layout, the planning of each individual scenic spot must be considered in terms of the overall look of the city. We must see to it that the mountains and rivers form a splendid contrast and set each other off magnificently. The hills along the Qiantangjiang River ought to be reconditioned, for the landscape here, with the river flowing at the foot of the hills and the lakes lying amidst the valleys, is certainly the most attractive of all the scenic spots in Hangzhou.

When we choose trees to be planted at historic sites, we must bear in mind the word "ancient". The archway on the Cool Hill in Nanjing has a horizontal plaque with the inscription "Relics of the Six Dynasties"[1]. Yet

1. The Six Dynasties: Kingdom of Wu (222-280), Eastern Jin Dynasty (317-420), Song Dynasty (420-479), Ji Dynasty (479-502), Liang Dynasty (502-557) and Chen Dynasty (557-589). All of them had their capital in Nanjing.

起座

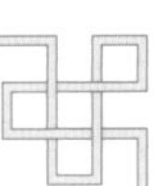

the passage within the archway is lined with deodar trees. Is it possible for deodar trees to have been planted here as early as the sixth Dynasties? It is certainly ridiculous to decorate Chinese historic sites with modern or western-style ornaments. The restoration of historic sites is not only a matter of repairing old buildings. The environment, the atmosphere, the decorations and furnishings should be appropriately set so that they are verifiable in historical journals. Otherwise, there wouldn't be any historic interest to speak of and such places would only present some sights.

The willows at Taicheng[1] are unyielding to the change of times;

1. Taicheng: name of an ancient city, originally the royal garden of the Wu Kingdom in the period of the Three Kingdoms (222-280). Its ruins are located near the Cock's Crow Temple in Nanjing.

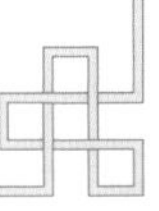

As of old, its ten-mile embankment is shrouded in a veil of green mist.

Who knows the implications of those lines? Men of today very often impose their likes and dislikes upon ancients. Some time ago, the residence of Pu Songling[1] was richly furnished like a manor house. If this old scholar had been alive, he wouldn't have been able to recognize his own shabby study. Luckily some people have undertaken to restore its original simplicity. They have certainly done a good thing.

With regard to gardens, preservation is more important than renovation. As to their trees, trimming of old ones should be given more attention than planting of new ones. In gardens with ancient-looking hills set against flowing waters and birds singing amidst a luxuriant foliage, the view is bound to be lovely in all seasons. In my opinion, stores and markets do not fit in with gardens. So when we set up stalls in gardens, we must see to it that no harm is done to the scenery. In garden construction, form must be considered along with function. In old times, the building of every individual pavilion, of every individual waterfront house, and of every bend in a long corridor was determined by actual needs. Both superfluity and ostentation should be guarded against. It is the same as writing prose and poetry, where any redundance is a flaw.

1. Pu Songling: 1640-1715, man of letters of the Qing Dynasty.

All branches of learning are closely linked with each other. Lack of careful arrangement in garden construction is much the same as lack of meticulous deliberation in writing, for gardens provide scenery in much the same way as writings convey ideas. That's one of the reasons why I say to construct a small garden is as difficult as to compose a four-line poem.

In his *Dividing up the Garden of Happiness*, Wang Shimin[1] wrote: "... It so happened that Zhang Nanyuan of Yunjian arrived. His artistry excels nature. He did his best to persuade me into constructing a garden. ...So, ponds were dug, trees were planted and a rockery was constructed. The project began in 1620 and lasted several years, during which period the garden was four times renovated. In the garden today winding flights of stone steps lead to the top of the rockery. Large ponds present beautiful scenes with their calm waters and surrounding luxuriant bamboo groves. The whole garden looks like a unified entity as if it were the work of God. Its cool galleries and bowers with deep recesses are appropriately located. Trees and flowers outside the windows set each other off. With all the lovely groves, ponds, galleries and waterside houses, the garden is beauty itself." In spite of Zhang Nanyuan's excellent artistry, the garden was four times renovated to attain its perfection. This is one more proof that garden construction must be conducted with great care. As often as not, renovations are necessary before perfection is attained. Therefore, at the initial stage, the designer should allow for possible improvements. In the appraisal of a garden, we must first of all consider its quintessence and then the time of its construction. It's the same as appraising an antique. However, all gardens must have at one time or another been renovated. That's why we must first of all look at the overall situation and then the separate parts. Forming a judgment by examining the separate parts without considering the quintessence is as erroneous as pursuing the trivialities while ignoring the intrinsic quality. No conclusion is possible with such an approach.

The fame of all great mountains, great rivers, historic sites and famous gardens rests primarily with their quintessence. It's precisely because of the full manifestation of the "quintessence" that the Five Mountains[2] have acquired worldwide fame. In making plans for a scenic spot, if the designer is ignorant of the importance of "quintessence", the project will definitely become vulgar in taste and consequently be a stain on

1. Wang Shimin: 1592-1680, painter of the late Ming and early Qing Dynasties.
2. The Five Mountains: Mount Tai in the east, Mount Hua in the west, Mount Heng in the south, Mount Heng in the north and Mount Song in Central China.

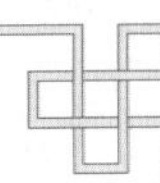

the holiness of natural beauty. I've been to several caves in Jiangsu and Zhejiang Provinces. In these caves the indefinable natural rocks are frequently cut into tasteless and even disgusting forms. So I've often cried out: "Give nature back to me." This is but one example to illustrate my point and I believe that you can see for yourselves the harm already done to these caves' natural charm. If one day people start erecting a lot of great mansions and TV towers, building highways and constructing midair cableways, the situation will be even worse, for such structures are destructive of the landscape's quintessence. We must be exceedingly scrupulous in this respect. Any indiscretion can result in a perpetual crime.

Gardens have their respective features owing to their different locations and climate situations. Each garden's distinctive style stems from the characteristics of its locality as well as from its own individuality. Even gardens in the same region may vary in style. There are urban gardens, suburban gardens, flat-ground gardens, hillside gardens, etc. Therefore, we mustn't arbitrarily make all gardens look alike. The culture and arts of a locality, its people's manners and customs, its flora and landform — all these may give variety to gardens. It's the designer's task to make the best use of these features. That's why the garden designer must be both ingenious and knowledgeable.

Discussing the art of painting, Yun Shouping remarked: "Charm lies in naturalness and gracefulness while interest stems from wonderful variations." This can also be applied to the construction of gardens and the arrangement of scenic spots. Nowadays, people tend to adorn a garden with too many scenes. This practice is bound to result in the loss of natural charm. Any unduly large-scale arrangement of scenes will only take from their fascination. Literary elegance is acquired through reading whereas a garden's interest is derived from its individuality. So much for my humble comments on the scenic spots I visited in my one year's rove.

Translated by Chen Xiongshang

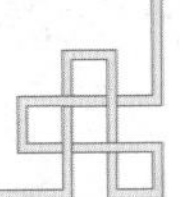

Part Five

Motion
AND
Stillness

I'd like here to elaborate on the idea of "in-motion and in-position garden-viewings", which I talked about at some length in the first of this series of essays, but which I consider not fully developed. Motion and repose are in essence relative in their relationship: there is no motion without repose, and vice versa. The same holds true in garden-viewing, where repose resides in motion and motion stems from repose. And from the interaction of the two an infinite variety of changing views and ingenious scenes come into being. This is what we mean when we say: once you understand the laws of change, you know the composition of nature. To a person sitting in a pavilion, the racing clouds and flowing water, the flying birds and falling petals are all things in motion; whereas to a sailing boat or a strolling person, the hills, rocks, trees and woods are all things at a standstill. Swimming fish in calm water is an example of the interaction of motion and repose, and beauty naturally results. Thus great garden scenes come from alternating angles of viewing between mobility and stability. "When looked at from a fixed position, all the beauty of nature can be appreciated, and the beauty of the changing seasons changes with the mood of man." This may serve as a generalization of the change of all things. A garden without water, clouds, shadows, sounds, morning twilight and sunset is a garden devoid of natural beauty. For these, though ethereal, set off the actual scenes of a garden.

Motion also exists in repose. Sitting in front of a rockery complete with horizontal and vertical holes, lively rock folds and dynamic shape, one would have an illusion of motion though the hill is at rest. The surface of water looks mirror-calm despite ripples. Likewise, a painting may look dead on the surface but is alive and moving all the same. A thing in repose is motionless if it is without vitality. Hence, we have the key to garden designing in the relationship between in-motion and in-position garden-viewings. Once this is understood, the principle of scenery viewing resolves of itself.

The feeling of material leads to actuality, whereas the feeling of colour is illusory. And the former plays a primary role if a garden is of genuine beauty. This is also true of sound architectural designs, which gain vitality through an adherence to actuality, and lose it if illusion is put in command. With the loss of actuality, a garden is reduced to a theatrical setting. And with calligraphy and drawing the loss of actuality will reduce them to mere printed matters. In the same token, the tawdriness of painted pillars and carved beams only serves to dazzle, whereas the

simplicity of thatched cottages fenced in by bamboos is food for soaring imagination. In *A Dream of Red Mansions*, there is a chapter entitled "*The Testing of Literary Talent by Composing Plaque Inscriptions in Grand View Garden*", in which Cao Xueqin commented on the spurious design of "Paddy Sweet Cottage" through the mouth of Bao Yu: "A farm here is obviously artificial and out of place with no villages in the distance, no cities nearby, no mountain ranges behind, no source of stream at hand, above, no pagoda shielding the temple, below, no bridge leading to a market. Perched here in isolation, it is nothing like a fine sight as the Bamboo Lodge which was less far-fetched. The bamboos and streams there didn't look so artificial. What the ancients called 'a natural picture' means precisely that when you insist on an unsuitable site and hills where no hills should be, however skillfully you go about it the result is bound to jar." By "artificial" and "far-fetched", the author hints at falseness, and by adherence to nature and natural beauty, actuality. Although it is only a passage in a novel, it is as eloquent and convincing as a scientific essay on gardening.

Guo Xi, an ancient artist, once said, "Water comes by its looks through

rocks" and "acquires its charms though being flanked by hills." Since ancient times, we have modeled our gardens on actual hills and waters, neither of which bears being treated in isolation. With this understanding of the laws governing the relationship between hills and waters, the designer will achieve his goal one way or another. A superficial understanding of the above quotations seems to point to an opposition of water to rocks, but the truth is that water changes with rocks and loses its shape and form in their absence. That is why in shallow water rocks are made to break the surface and in deep water islets are made to appear in their stead. Qixingyan at Zhaoqing in Guangdong Province is known for its grotesque crag and charming waters, where rocks and pebbles are faintly visible over the surface. The deep and quiet water caverns bend and twist in a variety of changing wonders. The crag, however, would be rendered inconspicuous and the banks formless in the absence of water. Therefore the two could never bear being treated in isolation, otherwise, we go against the laws of nature.

Since the interdependence of hills and waters is characteristic of a garden, it is of special importance that ponds be dug and water guided

in. In southern Jiangsu, the shapes of garden ponds are characterized by twists and turns, thus imparting a touch of femininity. In the Ning-Shao region[1], however, garden ponds are mostly square, presenting a geometric pattern of straight lines. Water by itself is formless; it assumes forms only when it is flanked by banks. Consequently, water inlets, dams and banks are the important means of lending forms to the water surface whether they are in a straight-line pattern or in snaky twists. As for the character of water in a garden, whether it is gentle or vigorous, calm or flowing, it is also conditioned by dams and banks. Delicate rocks miraculously lend a feminine touch to water, and rugged ones, a masculine vigour. Ordinary stones, however, must have clumsy shapes in order to be impressive. Grotesque and soaring peaks impress with their diversity. Moreover, ugly stones excel all other kinds with their uniqueness and originality. This is probably what we mean by beauty residing in ugliness. Just as stones are differentiated by their diverse characters of vigour, gentleness, beauty and ugliness, so is water characterized by unfettered vigour and gentle

1. Ningbo and Shaoxing, in Zhejiang province.

sweetness, but the latter's character changes with that of the former.

Waste gardens are not unworthy of visiting, and fragments of ancient texts are not unworthy of reading. As we all know that brocade and jade, even fragmentary, are precious articles, worth preserving, and difficult to part with. A poem by Gong Zizhen reads:

Unattained goals occasion unsettled hearts,
All the things are good that have missing parts;
Rhyming the glow of the sunset on the mountains beyond,
Human world is hardly free of human bonds.

The message of this poem should be kept in mind in garden designing.

"Spring witnesses the mountain looks, summer, the mountain mist, autumn, the mountain moods, and winter, its bony frame." "The mountain appears low at night, near when it's fine, and tall at the break of day."

All these views of the ancients are nothing but exhortations to put one's emotions into viewing a scenery, in order to make obvious the influence of the changing seasons upon nature. Building a landscape is a hard job indeed, but no less hard if your job is to enjoy it. "The flowers turn a deaf ear to the questions of the teary eyes," — bespeaking madness on the part of the questioner. "The spring breeze is interpreted as blowing endless regret," — evidence of melancholy on the part of the interpreter. Sightseeing, therefore, calls for sentiments. Only then will one be able to enjoy. A love for mountains and rivers, an acquaintance with springs and rocks, and the depth of one's aesthetic response — all depend on one's cultural accomplishments. Therefore, I would like to reassert here that enjoyment of a garden comes from a critical appreciation, and that without enjoyment, no good design of gardens will ever be possible.

Garden designing is a comprehensive science as well as art, dictated

by profound philosophies and capable of infinite diversity. To put it simply, it is to make poetic and picturesque sentiments, which are formless, externalize into waters, rockeries, pavilions and balconies, which have forms. Light and shadows, wind and rain, are all factors contributing to the kaleidoscopic change of views, not to mention the difference in geography and customs and habits. Moreover, with different garden visitors, the garden assumes different functions, which is an actuality never to be replaced by fantasy. It follows then that no good design of gardens will ever come of a disregard for their functions. Studying ancient gardens without a clear knowledge of the society and life of the time when they were laid out, and indulging in rash comments, like the Han scholars trying to interpret *The Book of Songs*, will inevitably lead to absurd and far-fetched conclusions. It is, therefore, of utmost importance that modern garden designs must not adhere doggedly to those of the ancient gardens. And to avoid getting into this set rut, a rich life and a broad-based knowledge will be of great help.

A landscape can be expressed in different brush strokes with different painters, and approached by different writers from different angles. Every actor enunciates in a way that suits him best, and every school has its own peculiar style. By the same token, a

garden can also be designed in different ways, and the peculiarities of each can be made manifest only through the depth of observation and the originality of conception. I was at first puzzled by the bright blue-green landscapes of the Song Dynasty with cinnabar as the base, red in colour, covered by blue and green. Then at the height of one summer I visited the Song Mountains in Central Plains, and found the topsoil red clothed in dark-green grass and trees, couched among which are houses and pavilions all with bright walls — a colour scheme that put me in mind of the landscapes of the General Li's, both Senior Li Sixun and Junior Li Zhaodao in Tang Dynasty. With heavy and thick colour tones, fair intensity and dazzling brightness, the aura of the mountains and rivers of Central Plains are brought out to the full. But the light green-blue landscapes of the south of the Changjiang River have a base of brown and grass-green, over which is applied a thin layer of mineral green and azurite, and with bare outlines of buildings tinged with a light brown,

they have a fresh and simple charm that is the blueprint for gardens south of the Changjiang River. Conception comes first, followed by coordination for harmony — this has been one of the artistic approaches since ancient times.

I've often said that the architecture and gardens of Suzhou are distinguished by a style of gentle harmony, and those of Yangzhou are mostly marked by its strength as well as elegance, just like the poems of Jiang Kui (about 1155-1209), who employed "a strong powerful pen in depicting tender feelings". Different as they are in styles, they all aim at preserving actuality and providing pleasing gardenscapes to people. Once the style is settled upon, then it is possible to deal with details and particularities, such as the proper localities for pavilions and terraced houses, the style for the rockeries and the particular pattern for streams and ponds. Everything must be planned out in detail before one could take full advantage of the terrain. And the scene-borrowing should be applied in such a way as to make it go harmoniously with the overall stylistic peculiarities. Nothing is done haphazardly, but everything has something to go by, such as the selection of rocks and flowers, and the choice of a mobile view or a static one. The designer, therefore, must proceed in a cool and unhurried manner, have everything at his finger tips, and then good work will certainly result. This is what we mean by conquering by momentum, the outcome of which will be a design complete in all its aspects.

Travelling in Fujian, I enjoyed its mountainscapes and found most of the peaks there bald and near-treeless, outcroppings everywhere, entangled by coiling and twisting ancient roots, which made the texture of the mountains so evident that it was almost possible to identify them with certain schools of landscape painters and the "light-ink stroke" methods they used to lend texture to the mountains. This is like perceiving the painter's approach through watching the material object itself, or like identifying the material object through the painter's approach. The brooks and streams in Fujian Province are known for their treacherousness and strong currents tumbling over projecting rocks, which, together with other features, provide an excellent model for landscape painters. But the cliff walls in Huizhou in southern Anhui and Fangyan in eastern Zhejiang simple defy any known methods of painters to make true-to-life pictures. With this kind of landscape paintings, different ways of "light-ink stroke"

will result in different sensations on the part of viewers, either of motion or of repose. The ancients loved rocks and meditated before cliffs in order to probe and get a revelation on the philosophies inherent in them.

In composing *ci* poem, great difficulties lie in the transition between stanzas, the words and meanings of which must sound at once coherent and detached. In designing and constructing gardens, attention should also be paid to the "transition", the skillful handling of which will enable a garden, even one with an area of a thousand hectares, to be imbued with a sense of completeness, and a lingering charm. The meandering gentle streams, the stacked-up rockeries and peaks, the storied houses and pavilions, and the trees and the flowers — none of them should be viewed in isolation. Transition is evident everywhere between split levels, panoramic vistas and zigzag views, and it is of great importance that these transitionary devices be handled with proper care. For example, corridors serve as a transition between storied houses and pavilions, and bridges as a transition for streams. The transition from bright to light colours calls for a middle colour to assuage the abruptness. In painting, we have reinforcing strokes to make the conception of the painter a continuous whole. Without transition, the garden suffers from inconsistency of conception and lacks exquisite charm. The realization of the ethereal and the actual depends, too, on the proper handling of transition. This done, the scenery will be endless and the charm infinite. It is essential that we should look for the ethereal in the actual, be alert for lingering sound at the end of a tune or of an instrument performance, and be good at detecting the minor while giving emphasis to the major. Is it not so that sometimes supporting roles exceed the lead? "The river flows beyond earth and heaven, the mountains shimmer between real and unreal." What is precious here is that nonexistence seems to get the better of existence.

A city must build gardens because they concern the well-being of

the city dwellers. The ideal execution of this task lies in "borrowing" and "separating". It is not impossible for cities to borrow scenes. The Three Seas of Beijing, for example, borrow from the Imperial Palace its lofty walls and turrets, its fine pavilions and imposing palaces. Another example is to be found in Li Gefei's[1] *The Famous Gardens of Luoyang*: "Looking northward, one would find myriads of palaces and turrets, towers and halls of the Sui and Tang Dynasties extending away for miles, a magnificent and colourful sight, and what Zuo Taichong (about 250-305), literator of Western Jin Dynasty, had spent more than ten years in praising and rhyming can actually be taken in at one glance." But it is something unheard of for gardens to have smoke stacks for neighbours and factory buildings for background. I regret to say, however, that this strange phenomenon is not lacking: today in Suzhou, both the Zhuozheng and Ou Gardens are glaring examples. There are also excellent examples of borrowing from out-of-city landscapes and distant temples and Buddhist pagodas. These are "borrowings". On the other end, there is "separating". Building city gardens, the designer must resort to "separating" as a means to keep out the vulgar and the ugly. Uniting and separating are relative in their relationship and complemental to each other. Without keeping out the vulgar, it will be difficult to introduce the elegant, and without obscuring the ugly, the beautiful will not be apparent. In a constructed scenery, the viewer is sometimes offered a one-side view and sometimes a two-side one. The crux of the problem lies in deciding on the proper choice. The Cuixiu Hall of the Yu Yuan in Shanghai is a building at the terminal end of the premises, with a market street at the back and a giant rockery in front. Staying in the hall, which nestles at the foot of the northern side of the rock hill, people will have no idea that they are in the midst of a noisy downtown area. With only a wall in between it seems as if it were a division between heaven and earth — an excellent example of "separating", which helps to bring out the effect in scenery-construction. Just as in a musical composition, a good garden also needs a prelude to introduce the viewer gradually to the main theme, which admits no shortcut or rash treatment. Full use should be made of the method of transition as I have mentioned earlier in this essay. City gardens south of the Changjiang River are seldom without a "prelude". There are people today, however, who seem to be favouring a direct approach lest the garden be passed by without being recognized as

1. Li Gefei: literator in Northern Song Dynasty.

one. Yi Yuan of Suzhou, which recently had a new gate built, is guilty of this blunder. But the Canglangting Garden, though only half open to the public, has its sceneries separated from the entrance by a stream, which serves as a "prelude" across which the strolling visitors must pass before they are led step by step to the climax — a real success.

Renovation of an old garden must be preceded by a study of its history, a detailed investigation of its present state, and an ascertainment of the date of the buildings and rockeries and their distinctive features. When this is done, then we can proceed to work out a refurbishing plan. For example, the mounting and repairing of ancient paintings, which is sometimes more difficult than creative work, calls for repeated deliberation, and each fill-in brush stroke must be carefully weighed before being applied to the original painting. Renovation of gardens should begin with the buildings, with carpentry taking the lead, followed by plaster work and masonry. Woodwork should precede the repairing of ponds, hills and the erection of peaks. The planting of extra trees and flowers can sometimes be carried out alternately. Last come road paving and wall mending. With the paintwork and the hanging of plaques, the renovation work can be considered completed except for the inner decoration, which is yet to be accomplished.

In laying out gardens, we may observe our ancient traditions, and may also learn from foreign designs. Neither approach should be rejected. It is the inevitable trend that the past and the present be combined and the past be made to serve the present. But it is not to be encouraged to copy indiscriminately from other people's works and knock together a plan haphazardly from other people's designs without a thorough study of their respective tastes and styles. A good garden designer must probe and explore the history and art of garden construction past and present as well as study the aesthetic thoughts behind the art, and the historical cultural conditions accompanying each stage of its development. Then every idea of our design will have a precedent to go by, and every achievement of our predecessors, both Chinese and foreign, past and present, will be at our finger tips. The ancients said, "It is more preferable to look at a painting than to copy it. With an authentic painting, we must study it in the context of history to see how it was conceived, whether it followed the right tradition, and to learn from its arrangement, brush strokes and ink-work, for there must be something I can learn from. And

as time goes by, my way of painting will automatically agree with that of the master." This assiduous way of learning is well worth recommending. Before the Meiji Reformation, the Japanese mostly learned from China; and after the Meiji Reformation, they modeled themselves on Europe, and later on the United States. But all the time, their architecture and garden designing have kept to the Japanese national style, or "the Japanese flavour", so to speak. This merits our close attention. Their study of history, of course, enjoys top priority as is evidenced by the collection in their libraries of Chinese tomes, the number and the variety of which are something to be wondered at. Take *Yuan Ye* for example. We regained possession of it only by copying from Japan. Moreover, a collection of books from Europe and America has also filled the stack rooms of their libraries from floor to ceiling. And such veteran scholars as Mr. Chuta Ito, Mr. Daijo Tokiwa and Mr. Tei Sekino have made a lifelong career of studying and investigating Chinese architecture, and their works on this subject enjoy very high academic reputation, testifying to their assiduous and sound scholarship and methodology. In order to achieve their goal, they proceeded from collecting a large amount of data, both first- and second-hand, and then narrowed down to the subject in mind. This is what is meant by "Other people's achievements can be employed for the attainment of our own goals." If "scene-borrowing" is important in gardening, then by the same token, borrowing ideas also features in garden construction as well as learning.

Just as in gardening, we have to deal with the ethereal as well as the actual, so is the case with our studies. So far I have written five essays in succession on Chinese gardens, amounting to tens of thousands of words. Now I feel drained and have nothing more to say. For half of my lifetime, I have travelled around, visiting all the famous gardens in China, and finally have come up with this long-winded talk, which, however, in large part derives from my actual experience. I now make bold to present my views with the hope that they would draw forth valuable comments from specialists in this field. Old as I am, my love for gardening remains as strong as ever. It is my sincere hope that once new ideas occur to me, I will pick up my pen to share them with you.

Translated by Xu Zengtong and Ren Zhiji

Author's Postscript

Between 1978 and 1982, I completed five essays in succession on Chinese gardens. These essays appeared in the Journal of Tongji University, in separate issues. Because of this, it was later found that speedy reference to them was out of the question. Further, the issues carrying these articles had one and all gone out of stock and yet people continued to come and ask for them. This led the editorial staff of the Journal to decide to make a collection of the essays, to be published for limited circulation, mainly within the school, to meet the needs of teaching and research work. It is now a couple of years since the decision was carried out and it seems that the reputation of the collection has grown with the years, as attested by increasing demand for it from various professions. The English translation of the five essays was done, in order of their appearance in the collection, by Mr. Mao Xingyi, Ms. Wu Yiyun, Mr. Sun Li, Mr. Chen Xiongshang and Ms. Xu Zengtong respectively, with editorial advice from Mr. Kong Fanren and Mr. Ma Wenyu. Looking back now at my humble work, I cannot help but be filled with the same kind of feeling as had made the poet Du Fu compose the following lines:

The master's interest has been aroused and the grounds are left untended.

Casually, I sat down, and found myself in the midst of berries and moss.

Written mainly on the impulse of the moment and not intended originally for publication, these essays can at best express only my personal views and sentiments to which I would like to invite critical comments, from all quarters.

Chen Congzhou

in his study in the spring of 1984

Index of Photographs and Illustrations

p. 15 & 16	Wangshi Yuan, Suzhou, Jiangsu Province
p. 17, 18-19	Zhuozheng Yuan, Suzhou
p. 20	top: Zhuozheng Yuan, Suzhou
	bottom: Jichang Yuan, Wuxi, Jiangsu Province
p. 21	Canglang Ting, Suzhou
p. 22	Liu Yuan, Suzhou
p. 23	Zhuozheng Yuan, Suzhou
p. 24	Qing Dynasty illustration of Yu Yuan, Shanghai
p. 25	left: Quan Shi Dong Tian in Yangzhou, Jiangsu Province
	right: Guyi Yuan in Nanxiang, Shanghai
p. 26	Liu Yuan, Suzhou
p. 27	Huan Xiu Shan Zhuang, Suzhou
p. 28	Shizi Lin, Suzhou
p. 29	Liu Yuan, Suzhou
p. 30	Zhuozheng Yuan, Suzhou
p. 31	top left: Tuisi Yuan, Tongli, Wujiang County, Suzhou
	top right:Wangshi Yuan, Suzhou
	bottom: Shizi Lin in Suzhou
p. 32	top: ZhuozhengYuan, Suzhou
	bottom: Shizi Lin in Suzhou
p. 33	Zhuozheng Yuan, Suzhou
p. 34	Qing Dynasty illustration of Dong Yuan
p. 35	Liu Yuan, Suzhou
p. 36	left & right: Zhuozheng Yuan, Suzhou
p. 37	Kunming Lake at Summer Palace, Beijing
p. 38	Qing Dynasty illustration of San Tan Yin Yue, the West Lake, Hangzhou, Zhejiang Province

p. 39 The West Lake at Hangzhou
p. 40-41 Xiequ Yuan at Summer Palace, Beijing
p. 42 top: He Yuan, Yangzhou
bottom: Shizi Lin, Suzhou
p. 43 top & bottom: The Slender West Lake at Yangzhou
p. 44 Qing Dynasty illustration of Baihua Zhou, Nanchang, Jiangxi Province
p. 45 Summer Palace, Beijing
p. 46 Li Yuan, Suzhou
p. 47 & 48 Wangshi Yuan, Suzhou
p. 49 top left: Wangshi Yuan, Suzhou
bottom left: Jichang Yuan, Wuxi
right: Liu Yuan, Suzhou
p. 53 Canglang Ting in Suzhou
p. 54 top: Zhuozheng Yuan, Suzhou
bottom: The West Lake, Hangzhou
p. 55 Liu Yuan, Suzhou
p. 56 top: Ge Yuan, Yangzhou
bottom: He Yuan, Yangzhou
p. 57 Zhuozheng Yuan, Suzhou
p. 58 Leifeng Pagoda, Hangzhou
p. 59 Qing Dynasty illustration of unknown garden
p. 60 Yi Yuan, Suzhou
p. 61 top: Ou Yuan, Suzhou
bottom: Qing Dynasty illustration of unknown garden
p. 62 Summer Palace, Beijing
p. 63 Zhuozheng Yuan, Suzhou
p. 64 top: He Yuan, Yangzhou
bottom: Ou Yuan, Suzhou
p. 65 Wangshi Yuan, Suzhou
p. 66 top: Yu Yuan, Shanghai
bottom: Summer Palace, Beijing
p. 67 left: Ge Yuan, Yangzhou
right: Yu Yuan, Shanghai
p. 68 Qing Dynasty illustration of Yeshi Yuan
p. 69 top: Qiuxia Pu, Jiading, Shanghai
bottom: The West Lake, Hangzhou
p. 70 Jichang Yuan, Wuxi
p. 71 Ou Yuan, Suzhou

p. 72	Zhuozheng Yuan, Suzhou
p. 73	top & bottom: The Red Plum Blossom Hall Garden, Changzhou, Jiangsu Province
p. 74	Liu Yuan, Suzhou
p. 76	Qing Dynasty illustration of Canglang Ting, Suzhou
p. 77	Canglang Ting in Suzhou
p. 78	The Slender West Lake at Yangzhou
p. 79	Yi Yuan, Suzhou
p. 84 & 85	The Slender West Lake at Yangzhou
p. 86	Wangshi Yuan, Suzhou
p. 87	top: Canglang Ting, Suzhou bottom: Liu Yuan, Suzhou
p. 88	Canglang Ting, Suzhou
p. 89	Wangshi Yuan, Suzhou
p. 91	Zhuozheng Yuan, Suzhou
p. 92 & 93	Summer Palace, Beijing
p. 94	top: He Yuan, Yangzhou bottom: Wangshi Yuan, Suzhou
p. 95	Liu Yuan, Suzhou
p. 96	Tuisi Yuan, Tongli, Wujiang County, Suzhou
p. 97	Shizi Lin, Suzhou
p. 98	Canglang Ting, Suzhou
p. 100	Shizi Lin, Suzhou
p. 102	Jinshan Temple, Zhenjiang, Jiangsu Province
p. 103	top left: Bixia Temple, Tai Mountain, Shandong Province top right: Tai Mountain bottom: Jin Shan, Zhenjiang
p. 104	Qing Dynasty illustration of Puyuan Yuan
p. 105	Yi Yuan, Suzhou
p. 106	Zhuozheng Yuan, Suzhou
p. 109	Canglang Ting, Suzhou
p. 110	Li Yuan, Wuxi
p. 111	Liu Yuan, Suzhou
p. 112	top & bottom: Zhuozheng Yuan, Suzhou
p. 114	Qing Dynasty illustration of Yu Yuan, Shanghai
p. 115 & 117	Zhuozheng Yuan, Suzhou
p. 121	Yi Pu, Suzhou
p. 122	Qing Dynasty illustration of unknown garden
p. 123	The Slender West Lake at Yangzhou

p. 124	Yi Yuan, Suzhou
p. 126	Yi Pu, Suzhou
p. 127	He Yuan, Yangzhou
p. 129	Tiger Hill, Suzhou
p. 130 & 131	Tongli, Wujiang County, Suzhou
p. 132	Tuisi Yuan, Tongli, Wujiang County, Suzhou
p. 133	top: Yi Yuan, Suzhou middle & bottom: The Pearl Spring, Jinan, Shandong Province
p. 134	The South Heavenly Gate, Tai Mountain
p. 135	The Eighteen Hairpin Bends, Tai Mountain
p. 136	Tai Mountain
p. 137	Swallow Rock, Nanjing, Jiangsu Province
p. 138	Liu Yuan, Suzhou
p. 139	Qiantang Jiang (river) in Hangzhou
p. 140	Qing Dynasty illustration of Liu Lang Wen Ying, the West lake, Hangzhou
p. 141	Zhuozheng Yuan, Suzhou
p. 142	top & bottom: Tai Mountain
p. 144	Tingfeng Yuan, Suzhou
p. 149	Yi Pu, Suzhou
p. 150	top: Zhan Yuan, Nanjing, Jiangsu Province bottom: The Slender West Lake at Yangzhou
p. 151	Zhan Yuan, Nanjing
p. 152	Liu Yuan, Suzhou
p. 153	He Yuan, Yangzhou
p. 154	Summer Palace, Beijing
p. 155	top: He Yuan, Yangzhou bottom: Zhuozheng Yuan, Suzhou
p. 156	Shizi Lin, Suzhou
p. 157	Yi Pu, Suzhou
p. 158-159	He Yuan, Yangzhou
p. 160	Zhuozheng Yuan, Suzhou
p. 161	Qing Dynasty illustration of unknown garden
p. 163	Shizi Lin, Suzhou
p. 164	Jingxin Zhai, Bei Hai, Beijing
p. 165	The Slender West Lake at Yangzhou

All the drawings were drawn in the Qing Dynasty.

Dynasties in Chinese History

Xia Dynasty	c.2100BC- c.1600BC
Shang Dynasty	c.1600BC- c.1100BC
Zhou Dynasty	c.1100BC- c.221BC
Western Zhou Dynasty	c.1027BC- c.771BC
Eastern Zhou Dynasty	770BC- 256BC
Spring and Autumn Period	770BC- 476BC
Warring States Period	476BC- 256BC
Qin Dynasty	221BC- 206BC
Han Dynasty	206BC- 220AD
Western Han Dynasty	206BC- 25AD
Eastern Han Dynasty	25AD- 220AD
Three Kingdoms	220AD- 280AD
Wei	220AD- 265AD
Shu Han	221AD- 263AD
Wu	222AD- 280AD

Jin Dynasty	265AD- 420AD
Western Jin	265AD- 317AD
Eastern Jin	317AD- 420AD
Northern and Southern Dynasties	420AD- 589AD
Southern Dynasties (Song, Qi, Liang, Chen)	420AD- 589AD
Norther Dynasty	439AD- 581AD
Sui Dynasty	581AD- 618AD
Tang Dynasty	618AD- 907AD
Five Dynasties	907AD- 960AD
Song Dynasty	960AD- 1279AD
Northern Song	960AD- 1127AD
Southern Song	1127AD- 1279AD
Yuan Dynasty	1279AD- 1368AD
Ming Dynasty	1368AD- 1644AD
Qing Dynasty	1644AD- 1911AD